PRAISE FOR
FOLLOW YOUR

"A breath of fresh air! Read it thoroughly and then recommend it to anyone looking for the secret to a more productive and satisfying professional and personal life."

AUGUST TURAK
Author, *Business Secrets of the Trappist Monks*

"This book is important on so many levels. Frank provides a compelling case to listen to your conscience. That's why you have one."

DR. MICHELE BORBA
Award-winning author of 22 parenting and educational books

"Love it! Buy two copies of this must-read book: one for yourself and one for your closest friend."

TED COINÉ
Co-Author, *A World Gone Social*
"Top 50 Social Media Power Influencers" — *Forbes*

"*Follow Your Conscience* offers valuable life lessons. Frank's words model genius. His values are brilliant and clear. His heart is profound. This book is so worthwhile!"

LOLLY DASKAL
Founder and President, Lead from Within
"One of The Most Inspiring Women in the World!" — *The Huffington Post*

"Inspiring! This book is like taking a deep, refreshing, and restorative breath. Frank's words help us calm anxiety and muster the courage and confidence to meet life's challenges."

MELANIE GREENBERG, PhD
Clinical Psychologist
Expert Blogger, *Psychology Today*

PRAISE FOR
FOLLOW YOUR CONSCIENCE

"This book opened my eyes, enlightened my views, and offered much-needed clarity and perspective. I love this book. I really love it."

LINDA ELLIS
Author of the world-famous poem *The Dash*

"A must-read for leaders and leaders to be. Sonnenberg proves that strong character will propel a career while weak character can torpedo one."

DENIS J. SALAMONE
Chairman and Chief Executive Officer, Hudson City Bancorp, Inc.
Former Partner, Member Board of Partners, PricewaterhouseCoopers LLC

"*Follow Your Conscience* reminds us to live a life of purpose and meaning. This book is a welcome read in our topsy-turvy times."

BOB MIGLANI
Bestselling Author of *Embrace the Chaos*

"If you think money is the only badge of success, perhaps your conscience can use a course correction. Frank provides valuable guidance on living life with a purpose."

BARBARA KIMMEL
Executive Director, Trust Across America — Trust Around the World

"Character matters! This book is as valuable to someone starting a career as it is to someone leading an organization."

FAISAL HOQUE
Founder of Shadoka, Author of *Everything Connects*
Contributor to *Fast Company*, *Huffington Post*, *Business Insider*

"I can't say enough about this book. I've read thousands of business and self-help books and consider this among the very best."

JOHN SPENCE
"Among Top 500 Leadership Development Experts in the World." — HR.com

FOLLOW YOUR
CONSCIENCE

Make a Difference in Your Life
& in the Lives of Others

Frank Sonnenberg

Printed in the United States of America.

ISBN-13: 978-1502345134
ISBN-10: 1502345137

CreateSpace, North Charleston, SC

Cover and interior design by Carrie Ralston, Simple Girl Design LLC.

To Kristine, John, Catherine, and Eric
— Be courageous, be kind, be humble.

And

To my wife, and best friend, Caron
— Still in love after 34 years.

CONTENTS

ACKNOWLEDGMENTS

I am so lucky to have wonderful people in my life who embody the personal values that are showcased in this book.

Ed Berryman is brilliant, has impeccable values, and has a work ethic that is second to none. Ed went through the painstaking process of reviewing each essay in this book and offered his thoughts. His comments were extremely valuable and insightful. Thanks for being such a good friend, Ed. You and Joanne mean the world to us.

Carrie Ralston is an amazing person and gifted art director. We started working together nine years ago, and I continue to thank my lucky stars. I've come to rely heavily on Carrie's creative genius. She continues to amaze me every day with her talent and good nature. Carrie created the cover and designed the interior of this book. She also designed my blog. All I can say is WOW! It's a pleasure and honor to work with you, Carrie.

Kathy Dix is knowledgeable, caring and absolutely extraordinary at her craft. Plus, she has a work ethic that's so hard to find these days. Kathy proofread this book and so much more. Her editorial comments and suggestions contributed greatly to the finished product. Thank you so much for your hard work and dedication, Kathy. I appreciate it more than words can express.

Caron Sonnenberg is my wife and my best friend. Caron served as a sounding board, reviewed each essay, challenged my thinking, and provided candid feedback. Her insight was invaluable. Thank you for your patience, encouragement, and unwavering support. This book would not have been possible without you, Caron.

Becky Robinson and her team at *Weaving Influence* helped me launch this book. They are a highly talented group of marketing and PR professionals. I've been watching them work their magic on social media for years. Now I'm blessed to be working with them on this book.

Eric Wagner is an extremely knowledgeable and hardworking IT professional who pulls all the magical levers to make our blog function smoothly. Carrie and Eric redesigned and upgraded the site earlier this year. Eric, I can't thank you enough for a job well done! You managed expectations, kept your promises, and made a tough job enjoyable. You're the best!

I am so lucky to be surrounded by positive influences in my life. Here are a few of them:

When I think of wonderful role models, my good friend Mark Sandberg PhD comes to mind. In my wildest dreams, I never could have imagined the impact that one individual could have on my life. Mark was one of my professors, and is the Founder of DAARSTOC, a leadership development program at Rider University. There is a saying, "The mediocre teacher tells. The good teacher explains. The superior teacher demonstrates. The great teacher inspires." Mark definitely inspired me. He imparted the knowledge, skills, and values that are so much a part of who I am today. If a person's life can be measured by the number of lives they touch, then Mark is the most successful person I know.

When I think about leadership, Dave Tierno, former Senior Partner, Management Consulting Group, Ernst & Young, comes to mind. Dave is one of the finest individuals I know. His emphasis on trust and teamwork in business, his strength of conviction to do what is "right" rather than what is politically expedient, and his ability to create a working environment conducive to excellence, all make him the very special person that he is. I thank Dave for his years of leadership, his personal and professional counsel, and for his friendship. I am honored and privileged to have worked for Dave for over a decade.

When I think about what success in business should look like, Larry Frankel comes to mind. Larry and I have been friends for over 30 years. It doesn't take much effort to see why he's so successful. He's brilliant, hardworking, and has unwavering integrity. Larry made it to the top of his field, yet he continues to remain grounded, humble, and selfless. Larry is living proof that good people DO finish first.

When I think about living the American Dream, my good friend Denis Salamone comes to mind. Denis was raised in a middle-class family where his parents emphasized family, education, integrity, and a strong work ethic. These values served him well as he worked his way up the corporate ladder to become a Partner and serve on the Board of Partners of PricewaterhouseCoopers — one of the largest professional service firms in the world. Denis never forgot his roots and remains humble for his good fortune. He and Jody continue to emphasize these very same values with their family. So refreshing!

My mother and father were wonderful role models who instilled the strong values in me that are so much a part of this book. My brothers and I grew up in a home where honesty and integrity presided over all else, where people's worth was measured by their character rather than their personal wealth, and where people got more joy from giving than from asking for more. My parents instilled in us the confidence that we could be anything or do anything, as long as we put our minds to it and worked hard to achieve our goals.

Being a parent to Catherine and Kristine has taught me the importance of having the proper balance in life — it's the moments in life, not the days, we remember — of recognizing the beauty in the simple things that we often take for granted, and of accepting the importance of living in the moment while planning for the future. Our daughter Kristine and her husband, John, married last year. Caron and I are so happy that John is now a member of our family. There's nothing more gratifying than watching your children lead happy and productive lives.

Caron is the love of my life. We've been married for 34 years and literally spend 24 hours, 7 days a week together. And yet, I never get tired of being with her. I've learned that life is much more rewarding when you can share every moment with someone you love.

Thank you all.

PREFACE

MORALITY: CHARACTER MATTERS

MORAL CHARACTER IS THE DNA OF SUCCESS AND HAPPINESS

Some folks have a split personality . . . on the one hand, they believe that being unscrupulous leads to success, but on the other hand, they also recognize that a solid reputation provides ancillary benefits. So they're ruthless most of the time and rely on a few PR maneuvers to promote their decency. In their eyes, moral character doesn't contribute directly to success — for them, strong moral character is a *sideshow*, not part of the *main* act.

The fact is, there's a direct correlation between moral character and success. We lose something very important when character is treated as an afterthought.

THE CASE FOR STRONG MORAL CHARACTER

Achieve peace of mind. People with character sleep well at night. They take great pride in knowing that their intentions and actions are honorable. People with character also stay true to their beliefs, do right by others, and always take the high ground. (So refreshing.)

Strengthen trust. People with character enjoy meaningful relationships based on openness, honesty, and mutual respect. When you have good moral character, people know that your behavior is reliable, your heart is in the right place, and your word is good as gold.

Build a solid reputation. People with character command a rock-solid reputation. This helps them attract exciting opportunities "like a magnet."

Reduce anxiety. People with character carry less baggage. They're comfortable within their own skin, and they accept responsibility for their actions. They never have to play games, waste precious time keeping their stories straight, or invent excuses to cover their behind.

Increase leadership effectiveness. Leaders with character are highly effective. They have no need to pull rank or resort to command and control to get results. Instead, they're effective because they're knowledgeable, admired, trusted, and respected. This helps them secure buy-in automatically, without requiring egregious rules or strong oversight designed to *force* compliance.

Build confidence. People with character don't worry about embarrassment if their actions are publicly disclosed. This alleviates the need for damage control or the fear of potential disgrace as a result of indiscretions.

Become a positive role model. People with character set the standard for excellence. They live their life as an open book, teaching others important life lessons through their words and their deeds.

Live a purpose-driven life. People with character live a life they can be proud of. They're driven to make a difference and to do right by others rather than trying to impress others with extravagance. (Sounds like a wonderful legacy to me.)

Build a strong business. Doing the right thing is good business. Everything else being equal, talented people would rather work *for* — and customers would rather buy *from* — companies that do right by their people, customers, and communities. While unprincipled business tactics may provide short-term results, it's NOT a long-term strategy.

CHARACTER MATTERS. IT'S THAT SIMPLE

Some people may say, "This stuff is naïve and wishful thinking . . . the reality is that business is ruthless and most people only care about themselves." These folks feel the only way to get employees to "do the right thing" is to coerce them.

I believe that's hogwash. When people are *forced* to "do the right thing," they'll try hard to fight and resist the effort. A better strategy is to prove that a strong character is in everyone's best interest — and it is.

Immoral behavior is *not* the easy road to success. In fact:

- People *without* character hurt themselves every day by losing the trust of their colleagues and damaging their reputations;
- Leaders *without* character squander the confidence of their constituents and lose the respect of their peers; and
- Businesses *without* character forfeit once-loyal customers and watch their most valued employees head for the door.

Most importantly, every day that you display weak character, you're letting yourself down. You must answer to your conscience every minute of every day. As Theodore Roosevelt said, "I care not what others think of what I do, but I care very much about what I think of what I do! That is character!"

STRONG CHARACTER IS LIKE A BOOMERANG

If most people know the difference between right and wrong, why do some shortchange themselves by selling their soul? They must think, "I'm under pressure to perform," "I don't want to lose face," and "I have an image to maintain." They reason, "The rewards are worth it," "It'll only be this time," and "No one will ever find out." Sadly, . . . they probably say, "Everybody does it" or "I've gotten away with it before. And I bet I can again." But, before you know it, this behavior becomes habit.

Well, if you look in the mirror and don't like what you see, don't blame the mirror. It's never too late to change.

It's not always easy to admit a mistake, persevere during tough times, or follow through on every promise made. It's not always comfortable to convey the hard truth or stand up for your beliefs. In the short term, it may not be beneficial to do right by your customers, to put people before profits, or to distance yourself from a questionable relationship. BUT, in the long run, doing the right thing is the clear path to both success and happiness.

When you have strong moral character, you'll be judged by who you are rather than who you pretend to be; you'll be a trusted friend rather than suspected as a foe; you'll learn from your mistakes rather than hiding them in fear; you'll serve as an outstanding role model for your admirers rather than leading them down a dead-end path; you'll look forward to the future rather than defending your past; and your reputation will do you proud rather than reveal your flaws.

Although you may not be able to quantify the benefits of being a good person, there's great truth in the saying, "Good people finish first." Strong moral character is like a boomerang that causes good things to find their way back to you — but it takes effort. Jim Rohn, the business philosopher, said, "Character isn't something you were born with and can't change, like your fingerprints. It's something you weren't born with and must take responsibility for forming." So promise yourself to be true to yourself and do what's right, even when nobody is looking — character matters.

THE TWO MOST
IMPORTANT DAYS IN
YOUR LIFE ARE THE
DAY YOU ARE BORN...
AND THE DAY YOU
FIND OUT WHY.

MARK TWAIN

PROMISE YOURSELF

Promise yourself to live every day to the max; To dream big and see every glass as half full; To set high expectations for yourself and for those around you; To get things done rather than talking about them; To say you'll try rather than complaining why you can't; To lead by example rather than through control; To win with integrity rather than at all costs; To make work fun rather than a chore; To face challenges head-on rather than surrendering your dreams to fear; To raise your hand rather than pointing fingers; and to learn from mistakes rather than covering them up. During your journey, promise yourself to do your best and nothing less; To make people feel good about themselves and proud of their accomplishments; And to be as excited about the success of others as you are about your own. If you promise yourself anything less, you'll be letting yourself down. After all, a promise is a promise.

Frank Sonnenberg

C H A R A C T E R
MATTERS

CHARACTER MATTERS

ATTITUDE

PURPOSE

COURAGE

AUTHENTICITY

HONESTY

INTEGRITY

HARD WORK

SELF-IMPROVEMENT

DETERMINATION

PRIDE

RESPECT

PERSONAL RESPONSIBILITY

LEADERSHIP

TOLERANCE

SELF-SUFFICIENCY

HUMILITY

GIVING

AMBITION

PASSION

HONOR

FAIRNESS

FORGIVENESS

FAITH

PERSPECTIVE

ATTITUDE

THE POWER OF A POSITIVE ATTITUDE

D o you think you're a positive person? A positive mental attitude can improve your health, enhance your relationships, increase your chances of success, and add years to your life.

The fact is, most people are bombarded by negativity each day. Sure, it's easy to cast blame by saying you're surrounded by negative people. The reality: A lot of the negativity is self-inflicted...influenced by the company you keep and your personal perspective on life's realities.

Take a minute...

Think how often in the day you're besieged by people who *argue* over money, *worry* about the possibility of failure, *complain* about someone's actions, *criticize* mistakes, *mistrust* someone's intentions, *blame* others to avoid condemnation, *envy* someone for personal achievements, and *gossip* about trivial garbage. (No wonder we're exhausted at the end of the day.)

Let's take a closer look at the negativity that we face every day...

Arguments. Many arguments are the result of poor communication, the lack of open-mindedness, or the clash of opposing values and principles. People also argue to force their viewpoint on others or just to let off steam.

Worry. Others worry about losing control. They desire certainty in an uncertain world. These people feel that worrying is productive, even though they'll be the first to tell you that they're driving themselves crazy because they can't get these thoughts out of their head.

Fear. Some people fear the unknown. Just as pollution damages the environment, fear is toxic to individuals and companies. Fear encourages people to withdraw, keep information close to their vest, hide mistakes, and refuse to take risks. Whether their fear is caused by something real or imagined, perception is reality.

Blame. Criticizing and insulting people in front of their peers, challenging their competence, demanding impossible deadlines, and cutting them out of the information loop are tactics that create negativity. Furthermore, when something goes wrong, people often look to others to cast blame. The result is that people usually watch out for #1 — themselves.

Complaints. The reason many people complain all the time is not necessarily because they're unhappy with their lives or circumstances. The fact is, compulsive complainers don't even realize that they're complaining. Perpetual complainers grumble out of boredom or a desire to turn an awkward moment of silence into a conversation starter. Or sometimes, people complain just because it makes them feel better to vent.

Criticism. There's a difference between constructive feedback and biting criticism. While constructive feedback is offered with good intent, constant and biting criticism can lead to stress, anxiety, and reduced self-esteem.

Mistrust. How much time is wasted and how much ill will created as a result of mistrust? People spend endless hours second-guessing intent, peering over shoulders, and creating elaborate approval processes to check and recheck.

Jealousy. When is enough, enough? We live in a society where many people aren't satisfied with their own accomplishments. If our neighbor buys a new toy, if our colleague receives a promotion, or if the TV celebrity flaunts a new design, we want it too. The problem is, after the excitement wears off, the finish line moves as well. Whether it's affordable, deserved, or needed never comes into question.

Gossip (our national pastime). People gossip to fit into a group, fill a void in conversation, prove that they're in the know, take revenge on a person, put someone in their place, or merely to gain attention. Gossip is a disease spread mouth to mouth. It's one of those distractions that keep us from focusing on our own lives.

IT PAYS TO BE POSITIVE

There's a direct correlation between a positive attitude and better relationships, superior health, and greater success.

A positive attitude can boost your energy, heighten your inner strength, inspire others, and garner the fortitude to meet difficult challenges. According to research from the Mayo Clinic, positive thinking can increase your life span, decrease depression, reduce levels of distress, provide greater resistance to the common cold, offer better psychological and physical well-being, reduce the risk of death from cardiovascular disease, and enable you to cope better during hardships and times of stress.

Here are several ways to adopt a positive mental attitude:

Surround yourself with positive people. Spend time with people who are positive and supportive and who energize you. Remember, if you get too close to a drowning victim, he may take you down with him. Pick a positive person instead.

Be positive yourself. If you don't want to be surrounded by negative people, what makes you think others do? Learn to master your own thoughts. For example:

- When you visualize a goal, it makes you more likely to take the actions necessary to reach it. Visualize yourself winning the race, getting the promotion, accepting the award, or landing the new account.
- Control your negative thinking. This can be accomplished in the following ways:
  - See the glass as half full rather than half empty.
  - Anticipate the best outcome.
  - Stay the middle ground. Don't view everything in extremes — as either fantastic or a catastrophe. This will help you reduce your highs and lows.
  - Mistakes happen. Negative people blame themselves for every bad occurrence whether it was their fault or not. Don't let this be you.

Consciously resist negative thinking. Be cognizant of and mentally avoid negative thinking. This will help you modify your behavior.

Be nice to yourself. Unfortunately, some people say the meanest things to themselves. If you criticize yourself long enough, you'll start to believe it. This negativity can drag you down over time. It may be time to fire the critic and hire the advocate.

Set realistic, achievable goals. There's nothing wrong with setting a high bar — unless you beat yourself up for not achieving your goals. The key is to build confidence by setting realistic goals and by hitting a lot of singles rather than swinging for the fences.

Keep it in perspective. Life is all about prioritizing the things that matter most in your life and focusing your efforts in these areas. This means that trivial things that go wrong every day shouldn't get you down. Learn to address or ignore small issues and move on. It's time to sweat the big stuff.

Turn challenges into opportunities. Instead of letting challenges overwhelm you, turn them into opportunities. (Rather than hitting the wall, climb over it or go around.)

Count your blessings. Be grateful and give thanks for the special things in your life rather than taking them for granted. Some people do this by giving thanks around the dinner table, keeping a written journal, or posting one special item each day on social media. Remember, some of the greatest possessions in life aren't material. Take every opportunity to make a wonderful new memory.

If you want to achieve happiness, better health, stronger relationships, and continued success, you may not have to look any further than the mirror. As the saying goes, "The happiest people don't necessarily have the best of everything; they just make the best of everything they have." Do you see the glass half full or half empty? True happiness may depend on how you view the world and whom you look to for inspiration. It pays to be positive.

A POSITIVE MENTAL ATTITUDE CAN IMPROVE YOUR HEALTH, ENHANCE YOUR RELATIONSHIPS, INCREASE YOUR CHANCES OF SUCCESS, AND ADD YEARS TO YOUR LIFE.

FRANK SONNENBERG

PURPOSE

LIVING LIFE
WITH A
PURPOSE

S ome people measure success by the wealth they've accumulated, the power they've attained, or the status they've achieved. Yet, even though they've reached success beyond their wildest dreams, they still have an empty feeling — something is missing from their life.

In order to fill that void and be completely fulfilled in life, their soul may be searching for something more.

Here are a few scenarios that describe this emptiness:

Lonely at the top. I was obsessed with making it to the top. When I arrived, however, I learned that it wasn't all it was cracked up to be. I now realize that my continual pursuit of advancement seriously compromised my ability to spend quality time with my family and build meaningful relationships with friends.

Enough is never enough. One of the ways I kept score in life was to compare my toys to my neighbors' toys. It felt good for a while, but each "high" just didn't last. I now know better. I realized that if I'm not careful, the game of life can become an obsession — there will always be people with more and less than I have.

Sold my soul. I would have given anything to be a success. I lied, cheated, and sold my soul to the devil. I understand now that although I've obtained fame and fortune, people don't like or respect me. Knowing what I've done, I find it hard to live with myself, and others seem to agree.

All work and no play. I was always the first person in the office and the last one to leave. While my business life has been a roaring success, my personal life has been a disaster. I realize there's got to be more to life. Balance matters, and I must be the one to make it happen.

Pleased everyone except myself. I never made a move without first seeking the approval of my friends and family. They're happy, but I'm miserable. I now appreciate that my opinion matters too, and counting on others to make up my mind for me is just a cop-out. After all, it's my life and I own it.

Lived in the future rather than the present. I spent much of my life thinking about what I was going to do tomorrow. Now that I'm older, I've come face-to-face with the reality that my days won't go on forever; I wish I had learned to savor every special moment as it happened.

If any of these scenarios sound familiar to you, it may be time for a course correction.

LIVING LIFE WITH A PURPOSE

Although everyone is different, there are common threads that bind a life with purpose.

Live by your beliefs and values. People who live a life of purpose have core beliefs and values that influence their decisions, shape their day-to-day actions, and determine their short- and long-term priorities. They place significant value on being a person of high integrity and in earning the trust and respect of others. The result is that they live with a clear conscience and spend more time listening to their inner voice than being influenced by others.

Set priorities. People who live a life of purpose identify those activities that matter most to them and spend the majority of their time and effort in those areas. Otherwise, it's too easy to drift away in the currents of life. As Annie Dillard, the author, once said, "How we spend our days is, of course, how we spend our lives."

Follow your passion. People who live a life of purpose wake up each morning eager to face the new day. They pursue their dreams with fervor, put their heart into everything they do, and feel that they're personally making a difference. As James Dean, the actor, once said, "Dream as if you'll live forever. Live as if you'll die today."

Achieve balance. People who live a life of purpose put their heart into their career and into building relationships with friends and family. They also reserve adequate time to satisfy their personal needs. Achieving balance means living up to one's potential in all facets of life.

Feel content. People who live a life of purpose have an inner peace. They're satisfied with what they have and who they are. To them, the grass is greener on their own side of the fence. As the saying goes, "The real measure of your wealth is how much you'd be worth if you lost all your money."

Make a difference. People who live a life of purpose make a meaningful difference in someone else's life. They do things for others without expectation of personal gain, serve as exemplary role models, and gain as much satisfaction witnessing the success of others as witnessing their own. As the old proverb says, "A candle loses nothing by lighting another candle."

Live in the moment. People who live a life of purpose cherish every moment and seek to live life without regret. They take joy in the experiences that life gives and don't worry about keeping score. Dr. Seuss may have said it best, "Don't cry because it's over. Smile because it happened."

START LIVING TODAY

The purpose of life is a perpetual question that has intrigued mankind since the beginning of human existence. Without purpose, it's easy to wander aimlessly through life instead of following your North Star. Without purpose, it's easy to squander your time instead of waking each morning with an unquenchable thirst to attain your mission. Without purpose, it's easy to achieve remarkable success and still feel that life is passing you by.

Success in life begins with purpose. When you achieve clarity, you'll gain a new perspective on your life. When you find your purpose, you'll feel good about who you are, what you stand for, and where you're heading. When you discover your purpose, an inner peace will replace the need to seek approval from others. And friends and family will begin to sense a new you: someone who is happy, motivated and self-assured — a person with a mission. People will say that there's something really special about you. And, they'll be right! As Robert Byrne, author, once said, "The purpose of life is a life of purpose." It isn't too late to start.

COURAGE

NO GUTS, NO GLORY

You're going to take the world by storm. You're talented and trustworthy, and you have a work ethic that's second to none. These words probably aren't coming as a surprise. You've already achieved a successful track record and have earned the trust and respect of your peers. Sure, you'll be faced with obstacles, slammed by adversity, and may even doubt yourself along the way. But I'm confident that you have what it takes to be a success. You're going to be a star. There's just one thing I'd like you to keep top of mind: Courage.

It's important for you to believe in yourself, stand up for the principles that you hold dear, and see the world for what it really is, not what you want it to be. Don't be afraid to embrace change, confront uncertainty, and face the unknown. For these things are ways of life. Make sure to be bold, follow your heart, and dream BIG. As Walt Disney once said, "All our dreams can come true if we have the courage to pursue them."

People with courage possess ten shared characteristics. They should remain as guideposts in your journey through life:

Self-confidence. Courageous people believe in themselves. They know who they are and what they stand for. They have strong values, recognize their personal capabilities, and are confident in meeting the challenges that lie before them. Courageous people are passionate and purposeful. You can sense courageous people when they walk into a room — they have a bounce in their step, maintain a positive outlook, and are comfortable in their own skin.

Conviction. You always know where courageous people stand. They're passionate about their beliefs and values and have consistent and predictable behavior. They don't blindly follow the crowd, waffle in the face of adversity, or change their opinion unless the change is supported by a strong, factual case.

Integrity. Courageous people know the difference between right and wrong. They don't just talk about honor; they live it every day by following the letter, as well as the spirit, of the law. They are trustworthy, objective, fair, and tolerant, and they stand up against injustice — backing their words with action.

Leadership. Courageous people aren't deterred by adversity or afraid of what people may think of them. Courageous leaders motivate people with personal charisma, expertise, integrity, and respect rather than by using their position or authority as a crutch. Courageous people are tough, but fair. While they may ask others to achieve the "impossible," they ask of others only what they're willing to do themselves.

Compassion. Courageous people put other people's needs ahead of their own. They know that the Captain must go down with the ship and that being selfless helps to gain the respect of friends and colleagues.

Objectivity. Courageous people understand the importance of trust, honesty, and full disclosure while confronting people who hide behind untruths. They believe that people are willing to make tough decisions if the options are presented to them in an open, honest, and objective manner. They also believe that people should admit their mistakes, learn from them, and move on rather than waste precious time playing politics.

Adversity. Courageous people aren't afraid of swimming against the tide or challenging the status quo. They stare adversity in the eye — running toward the problem rather than away from it. They know that saying "no" to one idea may enable them to say "yes" to another, and that old ways of doing things shouldn't stand in the way of a better solution.

Change Masters. Courageous people step outside their comfort zone to meet the challenges that lie ahead. They know that change is part of life and that some of the greatest advances have been realized by embracing change.

Embrace the Unknown. Courageous people follow their intuition. If information required to make a good decision isn't available, they follow their instincts.

Action. Courageous people put their money where their mouth is. They know that it's not enough to talk about doing something — instead, they act.

THE BADGE OF COURAGE

Some folks are afraid to take the risk of sharing their opinions or sticking out their neck for fear of getting it "chopped off." They think: "What if I'm wrong?" "What if it fails?" "What will others think of me?" So they spend their life playing it safe and trying to make themselves invisible.

These same folks are silent even though they have the best answer; they let opportunities slip through their fingertips even when they look promising; they see other people pass them by in the fast lane of life even though those people are less deserving. The truth is, they're so afraid of failing that they don't try at all — and consequently, they fail.

You have what it takes to be successful. So believe in yourself and your abilities or you'll never know what you're really capable of achieving. As Aristotle said, "You will never do anything in this world without courage. It is the greatest quality of the mind next to honor."

Don't be afraid to put yourself on the line if you want the rewards that life has to offer. That means, as in baseball, it's better to go down swinging than to be called out on strikes. Steve Jobs once said, "Your time is limited, so don't waste it living someone else's life. Don't be trapped by dogma — which is living with the results of other people's thinking. Don't let the noise of others' opinions drown out your own inner voice. And most important, have the courage to follow your heart and intuition."

Now you have everything it takes to be a winner. So go for it! Remember — no guts, no glory.

AUTHENTICITY

ACTIONS SPEAK LOUDER THAN WORDS

The car with a religious bumper sticker just cut me off. The parent makes the rules and then routinely breaks them. The leader just asked everyone to scale back and then spends like there's no tomorrow. The politician says, "Trust me," but we quickly learn that his promises are empty. The truth is, talk is cheap. Actions speak louder than words.

Why do people say one thing and do another? Why do they make promises one second only to break them minutes later? Why do people say they care when it's so obvious they couldn't care less?

Can't they see the potential damage to their credibility? Why would they torpedo a relationship that's taken them a lifetime to build? Don't they realize they're undermining their chances for success? The next time they say something, people may doubt what they say or second-guess their intentions — simply because they're no longer trusted. No one's going to stand up and shout, "You just lost my trust and respect!" but the silence will be deafening.

Some people may say it's not a big deal; everyone does it; no one's watching anyway; people don't really care. Well, I'm here to tell you they're sadly mistaken!

Let's face it, you send a message with what you say AND what you do. If words aren't supported with consistent actions, they will ring hollow. Someone once said, "Remember, people will judge you by your actions, not your intentions. You may have a heart of gold — but so does a hard-boiled egg."

Here are some examples of folks who live by the philosophy, "Do As I Say, Not As I Do."

ALL TALK, NO ACTION

The emperor is all talk, no action. Like the emperor's new clothes, everything is centered on the show rather than on substance. He talks a good game, but don't expect any action or follow-up from this empty suit.

The politician will say anything to win your vote of confidence; this person is great with words but don't ask for accountability. Once this opportunist gets what she wants, she's nowhere to be found.

The hypocrites are so full of @#%^*?! that even *they* don't believe what they are saying. Forget action on their part. They have a hard enough time keeping their own stories straight.

The drifters have no backbone. They make statements one minute and change their positions the next. If it seems that these folks are confused or evasive, it's because they are.

The professor speaks eloquently about theory, but that's where it ends. Action? That thought never crossed her mind. As the popular saying goes, "An ounce of action is worth a ton of theory."

The zombie is so oblivious to reality he doesn't even realize that his words are out of step with his actions. It only takes someone else to shine a bright light on this fellow to expose his insincerity.

ACTIONS MATTER: DO AS I DO, NOT AS I SAY

Whether you're a leader motivating the "troops," a role model influencing your "fans," or a parent showing that you care, it's critical to send straightforward messages. If your words aren't consistent with your actions, you're not only confusing the listener, you may also be causing irreparable damage to your own credibility.

Your reputation reflects the words AND actions that you send during the life of a relationship. In the early stages of a relationship, we extend ourselves in small ways and observe responses to our actions. Then we take appropriate action, engaging further or withdrawing a bit each time, until a level of trust is formed. Once we get to know someone, we look for regular and consistent patterns of behavior because the more predictable people are, the more comfort we have with them.

We ask ourselves: "Do they feel strongly about their beliefs one day and abandon them the next?" "Do they expect others to live by one set of rules while they live by another?" "Do they make promises only to break them?"

When you "walk the talk," your behavior becomes a catalyst for people's trust and faith in you. And it also emphasizes what you stand for.

The bottom line is simply this: Trust is not guaranteed, and it can't be won overnight. Trust must be carefully developed, vigorously nurtured, and constantly reinforced. And, although trust may take a long time to develop, it can be lost through a single action — once lost, it can be very difficult to re-establish.

So, any time you make a claim, no matter how small, and display inconsistent behavior, you shatter the comfort zone — and weaken your bond of trust with others. As a result, anything thought to be predictable in the future may be treated as suspect. The fact is, everything you do in life sends a message. So make sure to practice what you preach. As Ben Franklin said, "Well done is better than well said."

HONESTY

THE PLAIN AND SIMPLE TRUTH

What would happen if lying were the norm? Spouses wouldn't be able to trust one another; leaders wouldn't be credible; and the news would be meaningless. Everything, and I mean everything, depends on honesty.

The truth is . . . we can't build relationships if we mistrust what friends say; we won't follow leaders if we mistrust what they do; and we can't make good decisions if we doubt the accuracy of the information that we receive. Absent truth, instead of taking action, we'd spend our time looking over other people's shoulders, second-guessing their intent, and unraveling the facts from the falsehoods. The result is that trust is shattered, reputations are damaged, and suspicion rules the day.

So why do people lie? The reasons are countless. People lie to make themselves look better, steal the credit, cover up poor performance, conceal mistakes, deflect the blame, protect their reputations, and deceive and manipulate people. Regardless of the motive, the ultimate results are the same. As someone once said, "The worst thing about being lied to is knowing you're not worth the truth."

THE TRUTH IS NOT WHAT IT SEEMS, BUT WHAT IT IS

Dishonesty comes in many shapes and sizes. Of course, some people *lie in error*, in which they wholeheartedly believe their words when they're spoken. Others tell *bold-faced lies*, knowing full well that they're being deceitful. And still other people tell *white lies*, hoping to protect someone (often themselves) from the truth. Yet even though some of these folks may be well intentioned, it's all lying just the same. How do you identify a lie? As a general rule of thumb, if your ears hear one thing and your eyes see another, use your brain — because something is obviously wrong. Here are some common forms of dishonesty that masquerade as acceptable behavior:

Misrepresentation. Distorting facts to consciously mislead or create a false impression, spinning the truth, presenting opinion as fact, and using revisionist thinking or euphemisms to masquerade the truth are all forms of misrepresentation.

Omission. Leaving out key information to intentionally deceive someone. As Benjamin Franklin said, "Half the truth is often a great lie."

Fabrication. Deliberately inventing an untruth or spreading a falsehood such as gossip or a rumor.

Exaggeration. Stretching the truth to give a more favorable impression.

Denial. Refusing to acknowledge the truth or to accept responsibility for a mistake or falsehood that was made.

Lack of transparency. Withholding information knowing that full disclosure will have negative consequences.

Redirection. Deflecting blame to another person to prevent personal embarrassment or responsibility.

False recognition. Stealing the credit for someone else's hard-earned success.

Broken promise. Making a promise with no intention of keeping it.

Cover-up. Protecting the misdeeds of others. Those who provide cover for the misdeeds of others are as guilty as those who perpetrate the crime.

Hypocrisy. Saying one thing and consciously doing another. When words don't match actions, someone is being dishonest with others or themselves.

Bait and switch. Attracting someone with an exciting offer only to divert them to an inferior deal.

Living a lie. Pretending that you are something you're not.

Any way you cut it, when people distort the truth, they put their credibility at risk, while lowering their personal standards of honesty. Remember, BIG or small . . . a lie is a lie. Furthermore, a lie repeated many times doesn't change the truth. Additionally, one or many believers don't determine the truth or untruth. There's no excuse for dishonesty. None. As someone once said, "The truth doesn't cost anything, but a lie could cost you everything."

TRUTH BE TOLD

The value of honesty cannot be overstated. Every time someone lies, alarm bells aren't going to go off and that person's nose isn't going to get larger (like Pinocchio's), but something definitely happens. The question remains: Even though they fooled someone else, how do liars feel about themselves? The obvious truth is that they thought they didn't deserve the outcome or else they would have told the truth in the first place. They may explain away the lie by telling themselves that everybody does it or that the lie fell in a gray area. But I must ask you, is that any way to live your life?

When you stand for honesty, you believe in yourself and everything you represent. When you stand for honesty, everything you say carries the voice of credibility. But when you're dishonest, your soiled reputation will do the speaking for you.

There are several things you can do to demonstrate honesty:

- Think before you speak.
- Say what you mean and mean what you say.
- Bend over backward to communicate in an open and honest fashion.
- Simplify your statements so that everyone clearly understands your message.
- Tell it like it is rather than sugarcoating it.
- Present both sides of each issue to engender objectivity.
- If you have a personal bias or a conflict of interest, make it known.
- Tell people the rationale behind your decisions so that your intent is understood.
- If something is misinterpreted, quickly correct the record.
- Don't shoot the messenger when someone tells *you* the truth. Thank them for *their* honesty and treat the information provided as a gift.
- Willingly accept responsibility by admitting a mistake or an error in judgment — in a timely fashion.
- Hold people accountable when their words do not match their actions.
- Never compromise your integrity and reputation by associating yourself with people whose standards of integrity you mistrust.

The truth shouldn't be told only when it's convenient. Honesty must be a way of life. Honesty means that you care deeply about trust, cherish your relationships, and value the importance of a solid reputation. Honesty means that you try to do your best and are willing to accept the consequences of your actions. Honesty means that you respect others enough to tell them the truth and that you value your opinion of yourself enough to never live a lie. As the saying goes, "It's simple. Never lie to someone who trusts you, and never trust someone who lies to you." That's why it's critical to always tell the truth — or the truth will tell on you. Honest.

INTEGRITY

A PROMISE
IS A PROMISE

D o you think before you make a promise to someone? What if you can't deliver on your word? Does it really matter? The world isn't going to come to an end, is it? Well, actually, no — but have you considered . . .

Many people are pretty casual about making promises. As a result, promises are frequently made at the drop of a hat with no real intention of keeping them. "Let's do lunch," "I'll call you later," and "I'll be there in five minutes" are all examples of throwaway promises that are frequently made but seldom kept. However, this casual attitude can have real consequences.

When you break a promise, no matter how small it may seem to you, alarm bells aren't going to go off, but it can damage a relationship or your reputation. Think about it — when someone else breaks a promise to you, or gets caught in a lie, doesn't that make you feel violated or cheated? You can't help wondering whether you were wrong to ever trust that person.

Getting away with a lie can also be dangerous because it fools liars into believing they're invincible and that they have little chance of getting caught. Before you know it, lying can become a habit, forcing liars to spend precious time and energy keeping their stories straight. Once others learn about the lies, some people may forgive, but they surely won't forget.

PROMISE TO TELL THE WHOLE TRUTH

A promise is a promise. Some folks apply a rating scale, believing that breaking a *big* promise is inexcusable, while a *small* one is acceptable.

That's simply false. While breaking a big promise, such as failing to repay borrowed money, can torpedo a relationship, reneging on a small promise, such as being on time, casts doubt on future behavior.

Remember, trust is built through a series of experiences shared with others. When behavior is consistent, faith in the relationship develops. When promises are broken or people are misled, the bonds of trust are breached.

Broken promises imply that the offenders either didn't think before making the promises or don't care that they've let you down. They're also implying that their needs are more important than yours. So be careful about the promises that you make and with whom you make them.

Never promise the moon. If you can't keep a promise, don't make it. For example, you may not be able to guarantee someone a five percent investment return, but you can show them your track record and promise them that you'll work hard on their behalf; you can't guarantee that you'll arrive in two hours, but you can promise that you're going to leave at 10am; you can't promise anyone sunny weather, but you can promise to hold the umbrella open for them if it rains.

Some broken promises are excusable. If you can't deliver something on time because of an uncontrollable event, such as a family illness, most people will understand that the lapse was unintentional. On the other hand, breaking a promise intentionally (oversleeping) is different — you'll have to face the consequences.

When you distort the truth by exaggerating, spinning the truth, or withholding key facts, you also weaken your credibility for the future.

Half the truth is often a whole lie. Lying comes in many forms. Some people exaggerate or "stretch the truth" to make something look more attractive. Others "spin the truth" by presenting "selected" facts that support their position. Withholding key facts is also lying — it's clearly meant to deceive. When you tell a lie, everything that you say in the future may be treated as suspect. As Friedrich Nietzsche said, "I'm not upset that you lied to me, I'm upset that from now on I can't believe you."

When people are dishonest, they send the message that they lied because either they don't have a strong case or they have something to hide. Once they're caught in the act, liars will find that others may start requesting everything in writing, may start looking over their shoulder, and may question their motives. Most importantly, after they lie, everything said from that point forward won't carry the same credibility.

You're judged by the company you keep. When people cover for the misdeeds of others, they're as guilty as those who committed the crimes. If you're tempted to cover for someone else, first consider whether it's worthwhile to put your own reputation on the line for anyone who's undeserving of your good name.

YOUR WORD IS YOUR BOND

There was a time when keeping your word held special significance. We took great pride in being of good character. Personal integrity was both expected and valued. That was a time when everyone knew each other's family, and you wouldn't do anything that would cast a shadow on your family's good name. It was a time when integrity was instilled in children at a very early age and was viewed as instrumental in achieving success. The truth is, our world may have changed, but the importance of integrity has not. While we may not know everyone in our own town, the world is still smaller than you think. Create some bad news and you'll learn this for yourself.

Every time you give your word, you're putting your honor on the line. You're implying that others can place their trust in you because you value integrity and would never let them down. It goes without saying that if you don't live up to your word, you may end up tarnishing your credibility, damaging your relationships, and defaming your reputation. Most importantly, you'll be letting yourself down.

But . . . when you operate with complete integrity, what you say will be taken at face value, your intentions will be assumed honorable, and your handshake will be as good as a contract. Most importantly, you can take great pride in the standards that you've set for yourself and sleep well at night knowing that your conscience is clear. As for others . . . just when they think they're fooling the world, they'll realize that they're only fooling themselves. A promise is a promise, after all.

HARD WORK

EARNING SUCCESS THE OLD-FASHIONED WAY

S tarting a business is no picnic. It consumes your entire life for the first few years."

"As a medical resident, I've been working 15 hours a day, 6 days a week, for a year. I'm exhausted."

"When you 'hit the wall' during a race, it's really tough. Your head says go, but your body says no."

When you hear the words of a flourishing entrepreneur, an aspiring physician, a world-class athlete, or a celebrated musician, you'll find that they're likely to mention the hard work and personal sacrifices they endured in their relentless pursuit of success.

They may talk about waking up each day at the crack of dawn and pushing themselves to their personal limit. You'll forgive them if they boast about their "never-say-die" attitude, even though they may have been tempted to quit along the way. They might admit to the nervous feeling of putting everything on the line without knowing if their undertaking would ever pan out. Or recall the days when they were physically and mentally exhausted, yet they managed to find the perseverance and inner strength to endure. And of course, it wouldn't be surprising to hear that they had experienced failure several times before they ultimately achieved success.

These people persevered through so much — sleepless nights, time away from their family and friends, and possibly risking everything they owned. Yet, if you asked them whether they'd do it all over again, you'd hear a resounding YES!

Sure. They appreciate the blue ribbon, the recognition, and even the monetary rewards. But the ultimate prize is the satisfaction in knowing that they faced tough odds, gave it their all, and finished as winners. They deserve every reward that comes their way. Their success was earned.

Compare this hard-won success with someone who receives his or her reward through luck, inheritance, favoritism, or a handout. Or, more pointedly, by gaming the system, cheating others, or misrepresenting personal achievements. It was this very reality that moved author Sam Ewing to observe, "Hard work spotlights the character of people: some turn up their sleeves, some turn up their noses, and some don't turn up at all."

While they may have secured the trappings of success, they can't take pride in knowing that it was earned through hard work and effort. Importantly, according to research, people who feel that their success was unearned spent about 25 percent more time feeling sad than those who earned their success.

Here are some examples of success earned the easy way:

Easy street. Some people receive a job offer through nepotism or are granted a promotion because of friends in high places. Others strike it rich by receiving a BIG inheritance or winning the lottery. These people walk right to the front of the line with little to no effort on their part.

Winning the wrong way. Some folks never miss an opportunity to win at any cost. This includes cheating to get a good test grade, stretching the truth for personal gain, breaking a sports record using performance-enhancing drugs, or conducting business in an unethical fashion. I wonder if the prize helps them sleep at night.

On the take. There are people who take things that don't belong to them (no surprises here). This includes accepting an undeserved promotion or stealing the credit for someone else's hard work.

Winning on the backs of others. Some people feel entitled to a reward regardless of whether or not they've earned it. These folks revel in salary actions based on tenure or group membership, rather than on merit. When rewards ignore individual performance, the incentive to strive for excellence is lost.

Working the system. It's only reasonable that society provide short-term support to lift up the downtrodden. But this is in contrast to those who make a career out of receiving support. Government programs were originally intended to be a safety net, not a way of life. When we help people or organizations too much, we disempower them, rendering them totally dependent.

Hard work builds character, contributes to success, and promotes happiness. When people are rewarded for just showing up rather than for earning their way, it reduces confidence, promotes dependency, and robs individuals of their personal dignity.

When any part of the human body hasn't exercised properly, it will atrophy. This is also true of the human spirit —that is, people who are striving to achieve excellence. When we ignore the contribution that individuals make, it acts as a "demotivator" — killing their desire to achieve and making their organization, and ultimately their country, unable to compete.

We must celebrate not only success, but also the journey traveled and the signal accomplishments along the way. "I have learned that success is to be measured not so much by the position that one has reached in life as by the obstacles which he has overcome while trying to succeed," noted Booker T. Washington in *Up From Slavery: An Autobiography.* When you discourage individual initiative, you'll get less of it.

America is the land of opportunity. Our forefathers grew up with the dream that they could promise their children and grandchildren a better life than they lived. Today's children shouldn't expect anything less. Every generation has risen to meet the challenges before it. No one said it would be easy. Now it's our turn to rise to the occasion by celebrating and rewarding success. Earning it the old-fashioned way helps to make us great.

SELF-IMPROVEMENT

LIVE AND LEARN

A re you paid what you're worth?

Let's see . . . you'll probably compare the salary and benefits that you receive with the value that you provide to your organization. Right?

Did you ever consider how much you learn every day? Huh?

While money gets depleted over time, your experience remains with you for life. You'll be able to leverage that know-how into a better position within your existing organization or offer it to your next employer. That being said, investing in yourself may be the best investment you'll ever make. Period. And that begins with learning.

LEARNING TO LEARN

Learning requires more than attending lectures and regurgitating what you've heard. It requires you to be both teacher and student, to learn from books and personal experiences, and to be able to apply lessons learned to real-world situations.

Here are a few areas where learning can take place:

A new perspective. While memorization is often defined as learning, the practical application of knowledge shouldn't take a back seat. Rather than viewing things in isolation, we should learn to connect the dots and to discover patterns and trends. Instead of quick-fix problem solving, we should learn to address each problem's root causes.

And how! We currently spend the majority of our time learning "what and when." We should also focus sufficient attention on the process — "how" things are done. For example, it's critical to learn how to communicate more effectively, build relationships, establish priorities, increase efficiency, and improve our time-management skills.

A fresh look at life. We spend so much time running on the "treadmill of life" that we rarely have time to properly define our beliefs and values, short- and long-term priorities, and discover our purpose in life. Wouldn't it be a shame if we lived life on autopilot and then regretted our default path when it was too late to change course?

Make time for you. Many people take things for granted until they lose them. When was the last time that you took the time to learn about healthy living, reducing stress, or the best way to achieve work/family balance?

A NEW SCHOOL OF THOUGHT

Here are a few ways to learn:

Act like a kid. When we're young, we continually ask "why?" When we get older, however, we get defensive and feel inadequate if we don't have all the answers. It's time to learn like a kid again.

Broaden your world. Surrounding yourself with "yes" people is like talking to yourself. Listen to people with viewpoints other than your own. Try to see their side of the issue instead of living your life with blinders on.

Break out of the rut. Everyone likes routines. Learn by breaking them. Cover the same ground from different angles. Take a new route. Speak to new people. Get information from different sources.

Request feedback. Are you getting ready for a presentation or an interview? Don't be shy . . . request feedback from a colleague. Most people would be honored to help you. Remember, it's a lot better to learn in a non-threatening environment than when it's "game time."

Learn from mistakes. Do you have twenty years of experience or one year of experience repeated twenty times? If you're blind to your weaknesses, you may be repeating mistakes rather than correcting them. Remember, practice makes perfect — unless you're making the same mistakes over and over again.

Critique your actions. Football teams spend countless hours watching game footage to determine how to improve individual performance and build a winning team. Take the time to reflect on your experiences and learn from them. For example, ask yourself, if you had the opportunity to perform an activity again, how would you do it differently?

Increase your expectations. If you want to become a better tennis player, play with someone better than yourself. The same is true in other areas of your life. You're not going to improve if you don't accept challenges and learn from them. Step out of your comfort zone to "up" your game.

Success is a journey, not a destination. Winning is not a black-and-white experience in which losers explore ways to improve and winners receive a bye. Even winners should identify ways to improve on their performance.

LIVE AND LEARN

The great thing about self-directed, sometimes called informal, learning is that you own it. You determine what you want to learn, establish when the learning will take place, and have the opportunity to tailor it to your personal needs. There's no forced curriculum, there are no required exams, and there are absolutely no grades — except the ones you give yourself. Your only test is how much knowledge you're able to soak in and apply to your professional and personal life.

The world is at your fingertips. All you have to do is open your eyes and ears and begin taking it all in. The fact is, learning is as much an attitude as it is an activity. As the Buddhist proverb says, "When the student is ready, the master appears."

So promise yourself to begin today. Open your mind to new horizons — energize yourself by connecting with the world around you — and promise yourself that you'll strive for excellence. It'll change your perspective, it'll change your potential, and it'll change your life.

As Vernon Howard, the philosopher, once said, "Always walk through life as if you have something new to learn and you will." Live and learn!

DETERMINATION

DON'T QUIT – MAKE WINNING A HABIT

D o you know anyone pounding the pavement for a new job? Maybe you know someone who tried to quit smoking or you have a neighbor training for the marathon. How about someone who has received strict doctor's orders to eat healthier and lose weight?

Over the course of our lifetime, we'll all face situations that test our will, defy our determination, and challenge our character. Yet, even though our personal limits may be challenged, defeat should never be an option. Remember, even if life were a bed of roses, you'd still need to avoid the thorns. Of course, that's easier said than done — we're all human. Often it's so much easier to cheat "just this one time" or to give up entirely. Who will know? Answer: You will.

The fact still remains that the difference between a winner and an also-ran isn't always that the loser fell on hard times. Rather, the difference lies in how the adversity was faced. While some people stare tough times right in the eye, others are quick to surrender to a challenge. Which one are you?

ARE YOU READY TO MEET THE CHALLENGE?

Why are some people quick to throw in the towel?

Afraid to lose. Some people give up before they even start. Their rationale is "Why make the effort when the odds of winning are stacked against me anyway?"

Lack of reality. Some folks are like a "deer in headlights." When they're faced with a challenge, they're surprised, overwhelmed, and ill prepared to rise to the occasion.

Lack of confidence. Some people have a tendency to reach out for help as soon as they're faced with a challenge. The problem is, the more reliant you are on others, the less reliant you are on yourself.

Fear of accountability. Some folks leave their future to fate. They reason, "If there's nothing I can do to change the outcome, why even try?" Sounds like a recipe for failure.

Lack of will. Some people don't have the stomach to face adversity. They've given up so many times that they accept defeat without making an effort. That's when you look to a well-known song by the Rolling Stones, who point out, "You can't always get what you want, but if you try sometimes you just might find you get what you need."* Rock on!

BELIEVE IN YOURSELF

Are you up to the test? Although it isn't the first time you've faced a challenge like this, your body reacts the same way as before. It's like a physical and emotional tidal wave that slams into you. Your palms get sweaty, your heart starts pounding, your blood pressure starts rushing, and an adrenaline rush kicks in. "Come on," you say to yourself, "I've experienced this before." The million-dollar question is, are you going to face the test or throw in the towel?

I'm sure you see people every day who promise to go on a diet, eat healthier, exercise several days a week, or quit smoking. The problem is that they break their promise before they even finish their sentence. What about you? "This time it will be different," you say.

Don't let others tell you that you can't. What do they know? Don't succumb to the broad-based statistics. So you need a job? It doesn't matter what the national employment statistics say — you only need one job. Don't use other people as a crutch. Believe in yourself. You can do it. And please don't think your challenge is going to be easy. It won't be. If you set realistic expectations and follow a systematic process from the start, you can do it. You can win out over challenges that you face. Here's how:

- First, try to break BIG challenges into bite-size pieces. They won't seem as overwhelming and you can focus your energies rather than getting spread too thin.

- Then, rather than setting a long-term goal for yourself, create ambitious yet achievable, short-term milestones — quick short-term wins will keep you motivated. Make sure you celebrate every win. Don't spend your time complaining, worrying, or finding excuses. All that amounts to is wasted energy.

• And stop focusing on whether you've hit your goal. Instead, focus and measure all the positive activity and energy that you're generating. The fact is, if you're moving in the right direction, you're one step closer to your goal.

Now is the hard part. Take a deep breath. Close your eyes. Create a mental image of yourself achieving your goal. Remember, when the voice whispers, "It's time to give up," don't give in. When the voice whispers, "Go ahead, just one more cigarette," or "It's only one piece of pie," whisper back, "Not this time!"

All great performers, athletes, inventors, and entrepreneurs share one thing in common: They achieved greatness because they had the confidence, skill, inner strength, and determination to make things happen. Something inside them said, "I'm not a quitter."

GO FOR IT!

So reach deep down into your soul and give it all you've got. There are times when you'll reach your limit. Everything inside you will be telling you to quit. It's okay to take a rest to reflect on and celebrate your progress, and catch your breath.

You will be tested, but DON'T quit. Some people run into a wall and figure out a way to get around it. Other people brush themselves off and run into the wall again. What can you do better? What can you do differently to increase your likelihood of success?

Many people throw in the towel when they're on the one-yard line, not knowing how close they are to the goal line. That's the real moment of truth. Make the extra effort that'll put you over your own goal line!

While determination builds character, quitting is habit forming. When quitting becomes routine, you won't even think twice about giving up next time. On the other hand, when you overcome even an insignificant challenge, you'll gain the strength and motivation to confront your next challenge with confidence.

Isn't it about time that you believed in yourself? Prove to others and yourself that you have what it takes to succeed. You have the confidence, skill, inner strength, and determination to take on the world. So get ready for your next challenge. It'll be a whole lot easier this time. You're about to make winning a habit.

*"You Can't Always Get What You Want" from the album *Let It Bleed*, 1969. Written by Mick Jagger and Keith Richards.

PRIDE

IF YOU'RE NOT PROUD, YOU'RE NOT DONE

When we were young, we sought approval from our parents. As we grew older, we tried to impress our teacher, show off to our girlfriend or boyfriend, and suck up to our boss. Maybe it's time to impress the most important person in life . . . Yourself. Unfortunately, some people can't say that they're proud of what they do.

If you don't put your heart into your activities, if you hand in incomplete work as finished, if you don't do your best every time you start something, then you're doing yourself a tremendous disservice. The truth is, if you're not proud of what you do, you're not done. This doesn't mean that you have to win the race, secure every promotion, or be named Parent of the Year, but at least you'll know, in your heart, that you've done your best.

WHAT MAKES PEOPLE PROUD?

There are many things that make us proud — getting a promotion, making a difference in someone's life, buying a dream house, knowing that you're raising well-adjusted kids, or overcoming a serious challenge in life — to name just a few. These accomplishments are especially meaningful when they're the result of hard work, perseverance, and knowing that you've done your best.

But not everyone gets it. They sabotage their ability to be proud of what they do. The reasons are numerous:

• Some folks have talent, but they simply don't apply themselves.

- Others are so afraid of failing that they don't try at all — and consequently, they fail.

- Some people give up at the first sight of an obstacle.

- When brainstorming ideas, some individuals settle on the first answer — which isn't always the best one.

- Others are more interested in checking items off a to-do list, and moving on, rather than doing their best work.

- There are those who hand in unfinished work, and expect the recipient to review it for them — errors and all.

- Still others can't take credit for their achievements because they've cheated.

- Some people multitask or have so much on their plates that they can't give anything the attention that it deserves.

- Of course, if you receive handouts and didn't earn the rewards you enjoy, then it's tough to be proud of your effort.

- Some people measure success by being busy rather than getting the job done properly. Sure, they get a lot of stuff done — poorly.

You owe it to yourself to do your best in life. Don't wait to apply this principle to *big* things. It also applies to simple tasks such as writing a letter to a friend, working out at the gym, or spending quality time with your family. It doesn't mean that you'll always be successful. You won't. But at least you can take pride in knowing that you gave it your all. Plus, when you embrace this way of thinking, you'll end up raising your game by continually trying to better your best.

A TO-DO LIST TO MAKE YOURSELF PROUD:

Follow your passion. If you love what you do, you'll never view your job as work. You'll be excited to wake up each morning and give everything your best.

Never fear. You won't regret failing, but you may regret not having tried.

Compete with yourself. Forget about competing with others. It only breeds animosity. Instead, compete with yourself and find ways to improve your game every day.

Know your capabilities. Just because you're an expert in one area doesn't make you an expert in everything. Don't let your ego persuade you to claim an expertise completely outside your areas of knowledge.

Focus is key. Know your limits. Don't spread yourself too thin by biting off more than you can chew.

Leave your comfort zone. Set stretch goals that motivate you to challenge your best efforts. As Les Brown said, "Shoot for the moon. Even if you miss, you'll land among the stars."

Learn from the best. Identify role models from whom you can learn. Ask for feedback on ways to raise your game.

Practice, practice, practice. Excellence comes from practice.

Give yourself a report card. Learn from the past. After every activity, ask yourself, "How can I make it better next time?"

Don't quit. As Thomas Edison said, "Many of life's failures are people who did not realize how close they were to success when they gave up."

Don't let success go to your head. Celebrate success, but don't let it change you as a person. One of the most difficult challenges is to remain grounded after achieving success. Humility is a sign of strength, not weakness. People with humility are modest about their achievements, grounded in their values, and quietly proud.

Define happiness for yourself. Any piece about doing your best and being proud of what you do wouldn't be complete without a discussion about living with a purpose. Success in life begins and ends with purpose.

DO YOURSELF PROUD

Why do anything half-hearted if you have the ability to do it well? If you don't do your best, you're only developing bad habits, damaging your reputation, and letting your team down. Plus, you're robbing yourself of the rewards that you truly deserve.

You have what it takes to be a star, but it'll still take hard work to become a success. That means setting high goals, following ethical standards, focusing attention on your priorities, and sticking with it until you can be proud of your effort. So always give everything 110 percent. It's the extra 10 percent that everyone remembers. As Abraham Lincoln said, "Whatever you are, be a good one." And remember, if you're not proud, you're not done.

RESPECT

CAN
MONEY
BUY
RESPECT?

You may be an Academy Award winner, Super Bowl champion, president of a large corporation — or even the leader of a nation. But none of this automatically entitles you to respect.

And just because you're famous and we're members of your fan club, or we wish we could walk in your shoes for a day, doesn't mean that we respect you.

Some people believe that because they're rich, powerful, or famous, they deserve our respect — regardless of their behavior. Actually, nothing could be further from the truth. Respect must be earned.

DO YOU DESERVE OUR RESPECT?

When we were young, we were taught to respect our parents and siblings, teachers and elders, rules of the house and laws of the land. We were also taught to be tolerant of other people's ideas and respectful of their traditions.

As we got older, we became more discerning. Now we offer respect to people who behave properly on a consistent basis, and we shake our heads, often in sadness and pity, at those who think that respect is measured by the size of their pocketbook or the job title they possess.

The bottom line is that everyone is entitled to be treated with kindness, but that doesn't necessarily mean that they've earned the right to be admired or respected.

HOW TO GAIN RESPECT

So, how do you earn the respect of others? It's easy to respect someone who displays the following qualities:

Authenticity. You are proud of who you are and what you stand for. You're neither intimidated by someone else's opinion nor worried about what people think of you. You don't play games, have a personal "agenda," or pretend to be someone you're not. You're the real deal. Ahh, so refreshing.

Knowledge. You might be very smart, but you don't give the appearance of being a know-it-all. You're curious about the world around you, eager to learn, and hungry to improve yourself.

Integrity. You have high ethical values and are true to your beliefs. You follow the spirit of the law, not because you signed an agreement or are afraid of being caught, but because it's the right thing to do — and that's good enough reason for you.

Honesty. Your life is an open book because you have nothing to hide. You're passionate about being straightforward, and you're happy to deliver good news without sugarcoating the bad. You don't make promises lightly. In fact, your promise is as binding as a contract.

Fairness. You believe in building long-term relationships rather than settling for short-term gains. You strive for win-win relationships, knowing that if a solution isn't evenhanded, no one wins.

Tolerance. You are receptive to ideas, beliefs, and cultures other than your own. In the process, you always try to evaluate all sides of an issue rather than forcing your personal opinion on others.

Humility. You are modest about your achievements, comfortable in your own skin, and quietly proud. You shift your focus from taking to giving, from talking about yourself to listening to others, and from hoarding the credit to distributing the praise.

Selflessness. You give to others because you want to, not because you expect anything in return. You believe that your kindness helps to build trust, strengthen relationships, and enhance everyone's sense of self-worth — not to mention, adding to your karma.

Compassion. You go out of your way to treat others kindly even though you've reached the top of your game. You remember your roots and give credit to everyone who helped you along the way. You bring out the best in people in an effort to make everyone feel special, and you help those in need of a break.

Personal responsibility. You take charge of your life rather than feeling that the world owes you something. You set your goals high, make the commitment and sacrifice required to succeed, and accept the consequences of your choices. Of course, if things go south, you don't play the blame game or fall back on excuses — you remain positive and steadfast.

Quality associations. You are vigilant about the people with whom you surround yourself, knowing that you win or lose respect based on the company that you keep.

Organizations, like people, are also in a position to either win or squander the respect of others. For example, does your organization welcome anyone into its "tent" regardless of his or her behavior? Does it have an "everything goes" policy as long as it hits its quarterly numbers or beats the competition? When members do something inappropriate or unethical, is action taken — or does your organization "paper over" the situation, implicitly condoning the behavior?

RESPECT BEGINS WITH YOU

You may be able to fool others, but you can't fool yourself. If you want self-respect, it's important to set high *standards*, remain true to your *beliefs* and *values*, listen to your *conscience*, and never stop trying until you do yourself *proud*. Sure, you'll make mistakes and you may even fail along the way. But at least you'll know, in your heart, that you gave it your best effort and you lived your life the right way. And that has self-respect written all over it.

Now think about the people with whom you come into contact each day. Some of those folks demand respect because of their age, wealth, or position. Others feel entitled to respect because they're popular, have a big office, or because they've won awards. And still others think that everyone deserves respect regardless of their actions. The truth is, many of them don't even respect themselves.

It doesn't matter whether you're young or old, rich or poor, work on the top floor or down in the basement, everyone earns respect the same way. You can't require respect or demand it. You can't cut deals or take shortcuts. You can't buy respect or even place a price tag on it. And that's because respect is priceless. Earn it every day!

PERSONAL RESPONSIBILITY

THE BUCK
STOPS
WITH YOU

Personal responsibility puts you in the driver's seat to make the most of your life. You have the freedom to choose the direction that you want to take, determine the choices that you'll make, and decide how hard you're willing to work to achieve your goals. The key is to personally "own" your life, rather than abdicating the responsibility to others. The fruits of your efforts are yours as well, to keep or share, to invest or spend.

Personal responsibility needn't be a burden. It's a blessing when you assume complete responsibility for your life's successes and failures (and we all experience some of each). But hard work and commitment are required. If you want to lose weight, start with diet and exercise. If you want money for retirement, begin with a commitment to saving. If you want to be successful, you must possess the knowledge, character, and determination to win. Unless you believe in the tooth fairy, no one's going to wave a magic wand to make it happen for you (but that doesn't stop people from hoping).

TAKE CHARGE OF YOUR LIFE

Some people think that life is a spectator sport. They sit on the sidelines and expect to be rewarded for the hard work and effort of others. Of course, if something goes well, they line up to receive the accolades. And if things go south, they make excuses or find a scapegoat to take the blame. It doesn't (or let me say, shouldn't) work that way. If you're not willing to make the personal investment and sacrifices required to be successful, then don't complain if/when you don't achieve your goals.

The American Dream is built on a very simple premise: If you take a chance and you succeed, you reap the rewards of your success. If you take a chance and you fail, you have to face the consequences. Of course, there's no guarantee that just because you're willing to work hard for something, your success is a sure bet. But, by accepting ownership rather than abdicating your responsibility, chances are you'll get closer to your goals.

The fact is that the world doesn't owe you anything. If you want something in life, you must earn it. Here are some principles to get you on the right path:

It's your choice. If you want your life to be different, change it. If you're waiting for something to happen, it won't without your efforts. It's not enough to think about what you want to do (or worse yet, complain). Get up and do something about it! As someone once said, " 'I must do something' always solves more problems than 'something must be done.' "

Believe in yourself. One of the things that may be holding you back is lack of self-confidence. If you don't have the confidence in yourself, why should others? It may be time to invest in yourself so that you're proud of who you are and what you represent.

Raise your game. What additional skills do you need to achieve your dreams? Take an additional course, read a self-help book, find a great role model to emulate, and turn every experience, especially failures, into a learning opportunity. If you're not learning something new each day, you're becoming obsolete.

Actions have consequences. Think before you act. Then accept responsibility for your behavior. Do you intend to finish school? Do you discipline your kids? Do you listen to your doctor's advice? Are you saving for retirement? Do you text and drive? Do you blindly follow others? Remember . . . you own your choices. The decisions that you make have consequences.

Be accountable. Give everything 100% effort. When things go well, accept your well-deserved rewards, and when they don't . . . oh well. Don't point a finger if/when mistakes occur — admit fault, learn from your mistake, and move on.

Failure is a part of life. As Vince Lombardi once said, "It's not whether you get knocked down; it's whether you get up." Accept failure as a part of life.

Be self-reliant. Everyone gets into a pinch once in a while and may need a helping hand getting back up. That doesn't translate into a life of dependency. If you break a leg, use crutches for a few weeks to get back on your feet. But you shouldn't lean on the crutches forever.

"Don't drink the Kool-Aid." Some people see the glass as half empty. They'll tell you all the reasons why you may fail. The truth is, they're holding you back. Successful people face the same obstacles as everyone else, but the difference is in their attitude. Surround yourself with positive people; their energy is contagious. As James A. Baldwin, the American novelist, once said, "Those who say it can't be done are usually interrupted by others doing it."

You get what you deserve. People should be rewarded for exceptional performance, not for merely showing up. This provides an incentive for everyone to work hard AND work smart. Don't be satisfied to be a bystander in your life story.

It's your life. There's no such thing as a dress rehearsal. You can choose to make the most of it or wait for things to come your way. If you're spending your life complaining, making excuses, or pointing fingers, it's time to adjust course and accept responsibility for your actions. As John Burroughs said, "A man can fail many times, but he isn't a failure until he begins to blame somebody else." As with everything in life, you reap what you sow. The buck stops with you.

LEADERSHIP

COUNTERFEIT
LEADERSHIP

The responsibility of a leader is to lead. (What a concept.)

The fact is, some leaders are causing irreparable damage to great institutions by shirking their responsibilities. They're afraid to address difficult issues, make tough decisions, and introduce the change that's required to achieve long-term success. Instead, these "counterfeit leaders" spend much of their time playing politics, protecting their turf, and promoting their self-interests. To make matters worse, counterfeit leaders, in both public and private sectors, often masquerade as positive role models while condoning unethical or irresponsible behavior that undermines the very foundation of their institution.

With full complicity, we reward these misguided efforts by electing politicians for "life" and by paying executives zillions of dollars to damage the same organizations that they "swear" to serve. And just to show there are no hard feelings when things do go irreparably wrong, we offer many of our "finest" golden parachutes to make sure they have a soft landing into their next misadventure.

How do you spot a counterfeit leader? Here are some ways to evaluate yourself (or others) as a leader:

Are you a leader (in name only)? Counterfeit leaders take the easy road by accepting the status quo — even if they foresee difficult days ahead. They sidestep tough issues and kick the can down the road so that the day of reckoning falls on someone else's watch.

Vision. On the other hand, real leaders are visionaries with a "can-do" attitude. They take on the impossible, while their timid colleagues look for the exits. In the process, real leaders confront issues and obstacles head-on and make decisions that position their organizations successfully for the future. This means that their decisions won't always be popular, but they will be considered deliberate and fair; short-term results won't always be stellar, but long-term investments will secure a brighter future. These leaders won't always be loved, but they will be trusted and respected.

Do you take a strong stand? Counterfeit leaders evade decisions like the plague. They study problems, hire consultants, hide behind committees and task forces, and when in doubt, procrastinate — anything to shun accountability.

Conviction. Conversely, real leaders have a backbone. They make every effort to gather information, weigh alternatives, secure buy-in from their constituents, and determine the best course of action. Real leaders focus precious resources in areas that provide the greatest opportunity rather than trying to please everyone or making arbitrary, across-the-board decisions.

Where does the buck stop? Counterfeit leaders are masters at playing politics, finger-pointing, and finding others to shoulder the blame. They measure every action by protecting their turf and promoting their self-interests.

Humility. On the other hand, real leaders do what's right — period. Real leaders recognize that their stance represents something much larger than the whim of any one individual — as such, they put their egos and self-interests on hold. Real leaders do what's in the organization's best interest rather than trying to win a popularity contest, playing politics, or advancing their own private agenda.

Do you value integrity? Counterfeit leaders turn a blind eye to unethical behavior. To them, it's not how you play the game; it's all about winning. They believe that stepping on employees, squeezing vendors, or cheating a customer to make a quick sale is just the cost of doing business. In politics, running dishonest advertising against an opponent, sneaking through legislation in the wee hours, or sheltering a colleague from ethics charges is fair game. Counterfeit leaders believe the end always justifies the means — anything goes (as long as you hit your numbers or score points for your political party).

> *Integrity.* On the contrary, real leaders operate with integrity at all times; they are passionate about protecting their personal integrity and the reputation of their organization. They understand that trust takes a long time to develop, but can be lost in the blink of an eye. Real leaders know that instilling a strong culture and promoting ethical core values are instrumental for success. In fact, in today's turbulent times, everything is subject to change except an organization's core values.

Are you building a legacy for others to follow? Counterfeit leaders focus all their efforts on short-term success — at the expense of the organization's future. Shortsighted leaders skimp on R&D, cut spending on capital equipment and new infrastructure, apply Band-Aid solutions to serious problems, fail to develop key employees, and ram through major legislation without bipartisan support. Counterfeit leaders don't care about the future because they won't be rewarded for those efforts. Instead, the future takes a back seat to hitting the next quarterly bonus or winning the next election.

> *Credibility.* On the other hand, real leaders maintain a balance between short-term performance and building a better future. Real leaders know that short-term wins enable leaders to build trust, instill confidence, and maintain momentum. This provides them with enough credibility to make strategic investments and tackle the long-term challenges that ensure success. Real leaders understand the importance of motivating others to accept personal sacrifice to benefit others.

ARE YOU UP TO THE JOB?

Real leaders achieve success by setting the bar high, encouraging team-work, promoting win-win relationships, and demanding everyone's best effort. Real leaders win the support of their constituents by earning their trust and respect. This is achieved through powerful ideas, personal expertise, and impeccable integrity rather than through their position or by "pulling rank."

Real leaders set the tone from the top. They espouse a visible and meaningful vision that promises a better future than the prevailing conditions. The vision may be precise or vague, it may be a specific goal or a dream of a better future — but it must be attractive, realistic, and believable. A compelling vision provides direction, promotes excitement, and inspires commitment. Creating a vision, however, isn't enough. The vision must be brought to life and rooted in the culture. Real leaders never miss an opportunity to lead by example, serving as positive role models and reinforcing the beliefs and values of the organization.

Real leadership also means making hard choices, overcoming difficult challenges, and encouraging constituents to embrace change. Real leaders are not afraid to take a firm stance and accept responsibility for their decisions. In so doing, decisions are never made to win a popularity contest or to placate everyone by being all things to all people. Precious resources are allocated in areas where they provide the greatest good while carefully balancing short-term performance with long-term success. And, while you may not always agree with a real leader's decision, you'll always know that every decision was made in an honest, fair, and objective fashion. You'll never have to second-guess a real leader's intent; you'll know what he or she stands for.

All great leaders, whether in the public or private sector, make people feel proud of the institution they represent and realistic about the future. When a real leader promotes a common end, people begin to work as a team rather than at cross-purposes with one another. Self-interests wind up on the back-burner, while individuals begin working together for a higher purpose — the common good. And that, my friend, is what real leadership is all about.

REAL LEADERS ACHIEVE SUCCESS BY SETTING THE BAR HIGH, ENCOURAGING TEAMWORK, PROMOTING WIN-WIN RELATIONSHIPS, AND DEMANDING EVERYONE'S BEST EFFORT.

FRANK SONNENBERG

TOLERANCE

YOU'RE ENTITLED TO MY OPINION

So you're a vegetarian? Great. You go to the gym every day? Wonderful. You lost 14 pounds on your newfangled diet? I'm happy for you. You're voting for the Democratic (Republican or Independent) candidate? Super. You're a devoted person of faith? Good for you.

It's wonderful that you've assumed such a healthy lifestyle; that you're so passionate about your beliefs and committed to your causes; and that you want to raise your kids just like your parents raised you.

BUT . . .

But that doesn't mean I have to agree with you. Believe me, I'm not trying to pass judgment; quite to the contrary. Unlike multiple-choice tests, in life there may be two right answers to the same question. And I know what's right for me. I have strong beliefs and am passionate about my values, too.

I don't mind if you ask me to follow your lead every once in a while, but I'm afraid that you're misconstruing my silence (a.k.a. "No, I don't happen to agree with you") for an answer in your favor. And you're making me feel uncomfortable. So you're welcome to your own opinion, but PLEASE let *me* be *me*.

MY WAY OR THE HIGHWAY

On a small scale, forcing your opinions upon others can lead to arguments and damaged relationships. It can pit friend against friend, create strife among family members, generate tension in the workplace, and cause gridlock in government. On a larger scale, forcing one's values on others can lead to war.

The fact remains that if someone chooses to live a certain way, and it doesn't infringe on anyone's freedom, it's their choice to make. With that in mind, a true friend is one who respects a friend for who he or she is . . . not just if that friend shares the same viewpoints. It's important to be respectful of other people's ways of life and traditions — even if you're not in complete agreement.

Sometimes, however, it's not that simple — especially when one's beliefs and values encroach on another's freedom. In fact, some issues today are responsible for the polarization that is paralyzing our country's political process. Rather than striving to seek compromise, it seems that the new standard of discourse is "My Way or the Highway." This is a shortsighted and ultimately destructive attitude that is a "lose-lose" for everyone. We can't expect others to abandon their values any more than we would forsake our own.

The fact is, we live in a world that's getting smaller every day. It's important to be tolerant of other people's cultures and values, recognizing that no one has the right to force his or her way of life on anyone else.

BUILDING BRIDGES . . .

This does not mean that people shouldn't speak out for their beliefs. This process, however, must be civil and respectful of others' views. If we view every issue as a "take-no-prisoners" battle, or use underhanded (or dishonest) means to influence opinions, the outcome is likely to be ugly. On the other hand, if we're sensitive to other people's views and avoid forcing our opinions, then we're far more likely to achieve a satisfactory outcome and build bridges of trust.

Here are some considerations to promote an amicable debate:

GROUND RULES

- When a disagreement arises, all discussion should focus on the merits of each position, without denigration of others. There's no need to either disparage anyone or resort to personal attacks.

NOTHING BUT THE FACTS

- Timely and accurate information is an important ingredient of successful debate. As Daniel Patrick Moynihan once said, "Everyone is entitled to his own opinion, but not to his own facts."

- Does everyone view the issue from the same perspective? Is everyone taking the same short- or long-term perspective? Does the issue affect everyone the same way?

- Is everyone being fair and objective? Are people letting their personal biases influence their positions? Are unstated factors clouding their judgment? Is their bias based on uninformed or outdated thinking?

- Is someone trying to influence the decision? Does that person have a separate agenda or a vested interest in the outcome?

- Are any of the negotiators in it just to be "spoilers" with no real stake in the outcome, except to ensure that no consensus is reached?

THE BEST STRATEGY — WIN-WIN

- Many "battles" don't have winners and losers — there are just losers. Don't look for ways to back an opponent into a corner. Instead, find ways to let each side save face. You gain nothing by making others look bad.

- Take the high ground. Remain open-minded. Look for common ground. Identify ways to compromise and find win-win opportunities.

- Now hear this: Is everyone really hearing what the others are saying? Communication is a two-way street. It requires more than talking. Remember, there's a difference between listening and hearing.

- Although it may take longer, it's better to achieve buy-in than to be overpowering in order to achieve a short-term gain.

- Remember, if you win the battle (but ruin a relationship), what have you gained?

- Trust takes a long time to develop, but can be destroyed in seconds.

MAKING THE CASE

- It is important to put yourself in the other person's shoes. Try to find the merit in each other's arguments.

- Presenting both sides of an argument helps you to be objective and fair.

- Repeating something over and over doesn't make it true.

- Just because more people hold a particular view doesn't make it right.

- Raising your voice doesn't make an argument more convincing.

- Just because a person is silent doesn't mean that person doesn't have a message to convey.

- When you distort the truth, you weaken your credibility.

- Please don't dance in the end zone when you score points. It'll only damage the process going forward.

BE PREPARED TO HEAL THYSELF

There are a lot of good and decent people in this world who have much in common. They wake up every morning as proud parents and spouses. They build great businesses, give back to their communities, and assist those in need. They want to lead purposeful lives, provide for their families, and assure better lives for their children. It's important to build relationships on what unites us, not fight over what divides us. We should abandon the hateful rhetoric, expose our counterfeit leaders, shun our malicious role models, and reject the greed and envy that pits us against one another.

I long for a day when our leaders bring us together rather than divide us; when people strive to better themselves rather than trying to change others; when fairness and tolerance replace weapons disguised as words; when we measure success not by what people accumulate in life, but by what they're able to give to others; when "the world revolves around me" gives way to being a responsible member of the "world community." And when "win-win," long-term relationships define success, rather than winning at all costs.

Before we can make this a reality, keep in mind the wisdom of Bill Bluestein, the corporate executive, who said, "Before you try to change others, remember how hard it is to change yourself." But that's my opinion.

IF SOMEONE CHOOSES
TO LIVE A CERTAIN
WAY, AND IT DOESN'T
INFRINGE ON
ANYONE'S FREEDOM,
IT'S THEIR CHOICE
TO MAKE.

FRANK SONNENBERG

SELF-SUFFICIENCY

KILLING
PEOPLE
WITH
KINDNESS

O nce upon a time, there was a brat named Phil T. Rich. He grew up with everything a kid could want. He had every gadget imaginable, a house that rivaled the Disney castle, and parents who gave him free rein to do whatever he wanted. Unfortunately, his parents were rarely around for him — they had high-powered jobs, you know. And when they weren't working "killer hours," they were off to the club to play golf and trade gossip with friends. Phil knew that he wasn't like the other kids. Whenever he wanted something, he snapped his fingers and it appeared — like magic. He didn't have to work hard in school because he knew his parents would pull strings to get him into college and ultimately he'd be top dog in their business one day. The only problem was that Phil was totally dependent on his parents.

If the story ended here, you might be jealous. BUT, then it happened . . . Phil's parents thought they could double the size of their business by buying a competitor. While the transaction looked great on paper, in reality it had some serious shortcomings. And, before you could blink an eye, their entire business was on life support. Unfortunately, Phil's family lost everything. Phil thought he had it "made," but life as he knew it was gone forever.

Poor Phil. He was so ill prepared to face the "real world." While Phil thought he had the world by the tail, he was never prepared to earn the rewards himself. Unfortunately, this is a sad story without a storybook ending.

The motto of this story is that *"Helping people with too much kindness only makes them helpless."*

HELPING PEOPLE BECOME HELPLESS

Nonsensical no-bids. Some organizations offer sole-source contracts to a company rather than requiring a fair and competitive bidding process. This makes the supplier complacent and dependent, over time, never having had to win the business.

Guaranteed gratuities. Restaurant servers receive a 10% – 20% tip, regardless of the service they provide. This teaches servers that halfhearted work still gets a reward. So why try harder? Their complacency ultimately hurts the restaurant because a superior customer experience is built on the establishment's ambiance, food, and service.

Automatic rewards. Annual bonuses are sometimes based on employee tenure or "just showing up" rather than on merit. If high performers receive the same performance reviews and compensation that mediocre employees receive, then we shouldn't be surprised by complacency and apathy.

Gifts of graduation. Students are promoted to the next grade level regardless of whether they've met the minimum requirements. This "easy path" through school is sure to catch up with the students one day.

"Yes" — the most common cop-out. When we say "yes" to kids merely to placate them, or avoid a scene in public, they never learn the difference between right and wrong. Saying "no" to your children, when appropriate, is an act of love.

Unqualified quotas. If opportunity is provided to an individual based on special quotas rather than on his or her true qualifications, will this person use quotas as a crutch throughout life?

Questionable quid pro quos. Special favors doled out through nepotism or a quid pro quo rather than through earning a seat at the table have a real downside. Although these recipients may make it to the front of the line, the question remains whether they're up to the job.

Mediocre meritocracy. Some organizations fail to counsel mediocre performers. Mistakes ultimately become poor habits. Allowing employees to "get by" in this way helps neither the employees nor the organization.

Emotional excuses. Often, appeals are issued that encourage people to buy from a specific source (i.e., "buy American," buy union shop, buy local), regardless of the value offered. This may kill the incentive to be more competitive, only postponing the day of reckoning when value triumphs (as it commonly does).

Empty entitlements. Providing government services, in some cases for generations, rather than helping people to get back on their feet and provide for themselves is a sure path to dependency and helplessness.

Sometimes, well-intentioned plans have unintended consequences. We impose a mandatory gratuity so that the server doesn't get stiffed; we steer people to buy "Made in USA" because we're patriotic; we let the mediocre employees "skate" because they're the breadwinners for their families; we say "yes" to our kids because, you know, we're their parents and we want them to be happy. Even though our efforts may help the recipients in the short term, we are making them dependent on our good graces, rather than preparing them to accept personal responsibility for their future.

PEOPLE ARE NOT HELPLESS UNTIL WE MAKE THEM SO

When you look for synonyms for the word "dependency" in the dictionary, you'll find "addiction, habit and enslavement." When we encourage people to become *completely* dependent on the goodness of others for their livelihoods or achievements — when we reward people for lack of effort and personal initiative — we strip them of their confidence, trample on their dignity, and kill their will to improve themselves. Dependency purges people of their dreams, makes their spirit atrophy, and enslaves them to a lifetime of mediocrity.

We are compassionate people. We should make *every* effort to help the downtrodden get back on their feet, but we shouldn't absolve them of their personal responsibility to secure a better future for themselves and their families. As Congressman Paul Ryan once said, "We don't want to turn the safety net into a hammock that lulls able-bodied people into complacency and dependence." Phil T. Rich had the world handed to him, but when the silver platter was removed, he was unable to survive on his own. This story is only a fairy tale, but it's happening in real life every day.

Compassion shouldn't be measured by the size of a handout but by our ability to provide opportunity to reduce dependency, enabling people to become self-sufficient and helping them to realize their dreams. We must invest in people by providing a strong family structure and instilling solid values, a world-class education, and a powerful work ethic needed to succeed. Success also requires powerful incentives to those who make progress — and "tough love" to those who fail to make the effort. When we offer a handout, we may satisfy someone's body and soul for an instant, but when we *invest* in people, our action may benefit them for a lifetime. Bill Clinton said it well, "We cannot build our own future without helping others to build theirs."

HUMILITY

DON'T LET SUCCESS GO TO YOUR HEAD

Their stories are all too common: After years of hard work, these self-motivated high achievers reach the pinnacle of success that's so richly deserved. And — you guessed it; they let success go to their head.

These folks think they're so special. They buy expensive "toys" to show how successful they've become, and they push aside colleagues who've helped them achieve success. They abandon the values and principles that have made them successful. And worse yet, because they're successful in one area of their life, they come to think they're experts in everything. Why? They're so enamored with their own PR that their ego hardly fits in the room. Unfortunately, a swelled ego can cut short the payoff that these folks worked so hard to attain.

The simple truth is that not everyone treats success the same. Some people who achieve success remain humble, never forgetting who they are and from whence they came. The others? Well, we can learn from their mistakes:

FROM HUMBLE BEGINNINGS

Success is temporary. Success is a journey, not a destination. When you become successful, don't rest on your laurels. As soon as you take your eye off the ball, you risk losing your edge.

Stop feeding your ego. Don't isolate yourself from reality by building relationships with people who stroke your ego. Surrounding yourself with "yes people" is just like talking to yourself.

Compete against yourself. When you compete against others, it's easy to emphasize winning over self-improvement. However, when you compete against yourself, you both win.

Even experts have room to learn. Never stop growing. Know your limitations and admit when you don't know something. It'll help to keep you grounded.

Listen up. Discover what others have to offer and ask for their opinions before opening your mouth. It shows that you value their opinions as well as their insight.

No one's perfect. Be quick to apologize for your mistakes. You'll never learn anything or impress anyone by making excuses and diverting blame. And a little humility will remind you that you're human.

Share your success. You may be successful, but there's a good chance others helped you along the way. Find creative ways to share the credit and pull people up the ladder of success along with you.

Remember your roots. Remember where you came from and what you've learned along the way. Help others by mentoring them.

Get off your high horse. Treat everyone with dignity and respect. You may be successful, but that doesn't make you better than anyone else.

Bragging is ugly. There's a difference between excitement and bragging. We know you're thrilled about your new "toy," but others may be cutting back on their basic needs — be sensitive. As John Wooden, the legendary basketball coach, said, "Talent is God-given. Be humble. Fame is man-given. Be grateful. Conceit is self-given. Be careful."

Trust me. Money and success can't buy a person's trust or guarantee a good reputation. You earn these through your words AND actions. There's nothing more valuable in life than integrity. Trust me.

IN MY HUMBLE OPINION

Many of us come from humble beginnings. We make something of ourselves through pursuit of knowledge, integrity, hard work, and a bit of good fortune. Yes, people have every right to be proud of the success that they've earned. But that doesn't give them the right to be rude or disrespectful to others. As the saying goes, "Two things define you: Your patience when you have nothing, and your attitude when you have everything."

Some people, however, get a big thrill from boasting about their accomplishments or showing off their possessions. They've convinced themselves that they're better than others. The fact is, some folks let success go to their head, and they gain a weird satisfaction from pushing people around. That's wrong. On the other hand, just as it's disgusting for the "haves" to look down on others, it's equally disdainful for "have-nots" to resent those who've worked hard and have rightfully earned their success.

The truth is, all the money in the world doesn't make you a better person. It simply means that you have more money. Real wealth is achieved by appreciating what you already have in life. After all, money can't buy everything. It can't buy a close-knit family, good friends, a clear conscience, work-life balance, a happy home, a second chance in life, or good karma, among other things.

So don't let success go to your head. Be humble. Humility is a sign of strength, not weakness. People with humility possess an inner peace. They're modest about their achievements, grounded in their values, and they have nothing to prove to others. They're down to earth, comfortable in their own skin, and quietly proud. Humble people shift their focus from taking to giving, from talking about themselves to listening to others, from hoarding the credit to deflecting the praise, and from being a "know-it-all" to knowing there's so much more in life worth learning. There's no ego, no pretense, and certainly no gamesmanship. Humble people are authentic. As C. S. Lewis said, "Humility is not thinking less of yourself, it's thinking of yourself less."

GIVING

THE MOST IMPORTANT LESSON IN LIFE

S ome people have it all. They're talented, motivated, and know exactly what they want out of life. These folks want success so badly they can taste it, and their behavior reflects that drive. And yet, even though they have so much promise and so much to offer, this fairy tale doesn't always have a happy ending.

I'm sure you know people who fit the bill. Every step they take is measured against how they'll benefit personally; everything they do has a *quid pro quo*; and every conversation they have is steered to their favorite topic — themselves.

You can rest assured that when they call, it's because they want something from you; they use people as pawns to get what they want; they feel no compunction about being the first to take, then leaving the scraps for everyone else; they bully others to get more for themselves. Sharing? Giving? Playing fair? Not even on their radar.

In the short term, their charisma, talent, and drive earn them BIG kudos. Long term, they're disastrous. Their confidence is perceived as arrogance; their go-getter personality comes across as pushy; and their ambition is viewed as uncontrollable. The result is that their ruthless behavior causes them to forfeit the things they want most in life.

Fortunately, it doesn't have to be this way.

One of the most important lessons I've learned is that people who care about the needs of others and give of themselves go much further in life. "*Are you kidding?*" may be what you're thinking. "*That's the most important lesson?*"

Yes. Some people may believe that this philosophy is simplistic, naive, sappy, pie-in-the-sky, while others consider that it's only a nicety. You may be thinking, "*While that sounds great in theory, it doesn't work in the real world.*" The assumption people make is that you have to be ruthless to win. I'm here to tell you they're dead wrong. Here's why . . .

COMMON FALLACIES

Promote yourself to make a great impression. Self-promotion won't always lead to a favorable impression. In fact, the opposite may be true. If you want to make a great impression, spend your time listening and making others feel special rather than telling them how great you are.

You have to move fast to get what you want in life. Relationships are built on trust, which takes time to develop. When people are viewed as "a bull in a china shop," their motives are likely to be misinterpreted.

If I don't take it first, someone else will. When someone makes a concerted effort to be fair, others often return the favor. The opposite is also true — when someone thinks only of himself or herself, it breeds suspicion and contempt.

Packaging yourself is everything. When you work smart and provide significant value, you don't have to use gimmicks or play dirty to be recognized as a star. The best way to differentiate yourself or your organization is to be honest, caring, and hardworking.

Always try to get the upper hand. Relationships are all about identifying areas of shared interest and creating opportunities for everyone to be a winner. When someone gains the upper hand at the expense of others, it creates envy and resentment.

Don't compromise if you don't have to. Relationships are built on compromise. When you watch your partner's back, your partner will watch yours. Compromise is key. If two people are five steps apart, the best way to meet in the middle is for each person to take three steps forward.

In business, everyone's a competitor. Some people believe that the best way to propel their career is to outmaneuver their colleagues. But when you make people look good, you'll earn their trust and respect, and they'll be supportive of your efforts. Plus, they'll want you on their team.

There's not enough time to help others. When you make an effort to help others, you'll create an army of people willing to return the favor for you one day. But remember, please don't keep score.

THE MAGIC OF GIVING

You be the judge as to whether or not taking the high road leads to success . . .
Would you consider an egotist to be your role model? Would you choose a
self-centered person as a good friend? Would you recruit a selfish person
for your team? Would you marry and spend your lifetime with a greedy
person? I thought not.

It doesn't take much effort to show others that you care. For example,
treat them with dignity and respect; "make someone's day" with a few
kind words; provide encouragement; show concern; spend quality time;
listen with interest; share half; put their needs before your own; reach
out to someone in need; share your wisdom and experience; pay them
a compliment; teach them how to fish for a lifetime; thank someone for
an effort well done; ask for or share an honest opinion; show gratitude;
remember a special event; instill a strong set of values; provide encouragement.

Remember . . . give because you want to, not because you must. That way,
it's from your heart. Believe me, it will come back to you in ways you'd
never imagine — but don't give because you're expecting something in return.

Some people may look at you cross-eyed after you make a kind gesture.
"*C'mon*," they'll think, "*why are you really doing this? No one does something for nothing.*" Then, when they realize there's no catch, something
magical will happen. You'll be viewed in an entirely new light.

Just think how far your kindness will go toward building trust, strengthening
your relationships, developing teamwork and camaraderie, enhancing your
reputation and sense of self-worth — not to mention, adding to your karma.

Giving is a winning game. As Patti Thor, the best-selling author says, "It's
not that successful people are givers; it is that givers are successful people."
So remember, it IS better to give than receive. Go ahead; give it a try.

AMBITION

THERE'S MORE TO LIFE THAN MONEY

I t's easy to know how well you did in school, the baseball game, or even at work. But how do you grade success in life?

In school we receive grades; in baseball we count runs; and at work we get performance reviews. But life isn't quite that simple. We may ask ourselves: "Do I have more good days or bad days? Am I doing better today than yesterday? Do I give more than I take? Am I doing better or worse than others?"

At the end of a day, we may say: "Three people smiled at me; someone thanked me for doing them a favor; and my kids told me they loved me." Not bad.

But . . . it's really hard to put a figure on intangibles such as a smile, a thank you, and the love of our children. And because these intangibles are difficult to quantify (and frequently not in the public eye), we often discount their true worth. Instead, we turn to more recognizable ways to measure success — *money and the things it can buy.*

And why not?

Money is tangible. You can feel it. You can count it. You can flaunt it. You can use it to impress others, while impressing yourself.

Money is flexible. You can save it or spend it. You can buy something for yourself or a friend. Or, you can invest your money and hopefully turn it into more money.

Money spells success. (Or does it?) It's tempting to assume that if we have a better car, a bigger house, and take more vacations, we're leading "the good life." But are we leading a meaningful life?

The truth is, money can't buy everything. For example, money can't buy peace of mind, good friends, a close-knit family, work-life balance, a worry-free day, good karma, time to relax, good health, a golden anniversary, quality time with your kids, a new beginning, natural beauty, happy memories, to name just a few. Many people are actually poor because the only thing they have is money.

IF YOU LIVE FOR MONEY, IT'S TIME TO GET A LIFE

Are you willing to sacrifice your dreams for more money? Some folks justify continuing in a miserable job situation by acknowledging that they're well compensated. People who live a life of purpose wake up each morning excited to pursue their dreams and make a difference. — Money can't guarantee that.

Are you willing to compromise your honor for more money? Everything has a price, but not everything should be for sale. Some folks make money by being ruthless or doing unscrupulous things. People with a clear conscience have core beliefs and values that influence their decisions, shape their day-to-day actions, and determine their short- and long-term priorities. The result is that they spend more time listening to their inner voice. — Chances are, they sleep well at night.

Are you willing to squander your happiness for more money? Some people don't understand the meaning of enough. They think the grass is always greener on their neighbor's side of the fence. Others understand the difference between wanting and needing. As the Yiddish proverb says, "The truly rich are those who enjoy what they have." — Nowhere in the proverb is the word money mentioned.

Are you willing to forgo relationships for more money? Think about "the takers." You know them. They measure every action by how much they will personally benefit, while "the givers" do things without expectation of personal gain. — Which are you?

Are you willing to compromise quality of life for more money? Some people eye a prize without considering the sacrifices required to achieve it. Success has its own tradeoffs. It may demand long hours, time away from family or a significant financial commitment. The key is to understand the requirements for success before embarking on your journey. — Choose wisely.

Are you willing to forgo peace of mind for more money? There are those who feel that happiness lies in having more. So they never have enough. As a consequence, they set very high expectations and are constantly worried and stressed out. — Do you call that happiness?

Are you willing to miss out on life for more money? Some people don't take time to smell the roses. It's hard to calculate the value of memories, such as a clean bill of health, first kiss, grandchildren, passing the driver's test, acceptance letter, visit from the tooth fairy, cheers from the crowd, retirement, "Mama . . . Dada," bedtime stories, potty training, and "I love you, too." It's important to focus on the journey as well the destination. — There's no dress rehearsal in life.

Are you willing to cash in your personal dignity for more money? Some people are consumed with seeking the approval of others. The most important person to satisfy, however, is you. It's your life. So do your best. Be your own person. And remember, you're not finished until you do yourself proud. As the author John Mason said, "You were born an original. Don't die a copy." — It's time to be the real you.

MONEY . . . WHAT'S IT ALL WORTH?

I'm not saying that money isn't important. Rather, this is a plea to acknowledge that there's more to life than money. As Garth Brooks, the American country music singer, said, "You aren't wealthy until you have something money can't buy." So we must assign appropriate value to the intangible areas of our lives, such as our honor, personal relationships, peace of mind, and quality family time, to name a few examples. If we take these things for granted, and lose them as a result, we are on the road to personal bankruptcy.

It's important to keep money in perspective. Do you spend more money satisfying your desires than fulfilling your needs? Do you let money dictate your activities, affect your relationships, and consume your thoughts? Is money a constant cause of anxiety and a source of stress? If you answer yes to these questions, you may be becoming a slave to your money.

When you look back on your life, will you gauge success by the power that you attained and the wealth that you accumulated? Or will you measure the degree to which your life was rich in character and purpose? Will it matter that you led an honorable existence, made a difference in people's lives, and left the world a better place for your children? Albert Einstein said it well, "Not everything that can be counted counts, and not everything that counts can be counted." The choice is yours. There's more to life than money.

PASSION

LOST AND FOUND

Passion is about more than finding your calling in life. It means caring intensely about who you are, what you stand for, and what you do every day. It's about making a difference in people's lives, pursuing your dreams, and contributing to the world around you. Passion is about waking up with a purpose, following your heart, and living life to the fullest. As Mae West said, "You only live once, but if you do it right, once is enough." So find your passion and live your life with gusto.

Sadly, some folks don't live . . . they merely exist. They sit silently rather than taking a stand; they follow blindly rather than thinking for themselves; and they dip their toes in the water rather than taking the plunge. These folks are self-conscious about "standing out," afraid of making a commitment, uncomfortable in their own skin, and reluctant to put themselves on the line. They're a bit like wallpaper, comfortable living life in the background despite the fact that they're bursting with promise. So, what are you waiting for? It's time to get going and pursue your passion. As Lucille Ball said, "I'd rather regret the things I've done than regret the things I haven't done."

WHERE IS PASSION BORN?

If you're passionate about something, you'll wake up each morning thrilled to greet another day. You'll require less sleep; you may forget to eat; and you'll always make time for the things you love. In fact, some folks find it hard to stop thinking about anything else. But who's even trying? When you're passionate about something, the adrenaline rush will consume you from the top of your head to the tip of your toes. And you may smile so much that your jaw hurts. People will say your excitement is contagious and that you look happier than ever. The truth is, you are.

DISCOVER YOUR PASSION:

Toast yourself. Pretend you're toasting yourself at your future retirement dinner. What were the most fulfilling moments of your life? What made you happiest? Then make sure you do more of those things before your real retirement.

Get free advice. Ask some retired people what changes they'd make if they had the opportunity to live life over again. Learn from their experience.

Think out of the box. Assume that you have enough money and that only your *wishes* matter — if you had only 10 years to live, what would you do? Once you've identified some possibilities, get moving!

BELIEVE IN YOURSELF:

Confidence matters. If you don't have confidence in yourself, don't expect others to have faith in you.

Kill negative thoughts. Banish those negative thoughts. They'll reduce your confidence and drag you down.

Accentuate the positive. Surround yourself with people who provide encouragement. They'll also provide energy and support when you need it most.

See yourself a success. Spend a few moments each day picturing yourself a success. Imagine yourself accepting the award, closing the big deal, or receiving a standing ovation for your achievements. It might just happen!

TAKE A CHANCE:

What's worse — failing or never trying? When you attempt something, there are two outcomes — success or failure. If you don't try, you give up any opportunity for success. As Wayne Gretzky said, "You miss 100% of the shots you don't take."

What's the worst that could happen? Some efforts seem daunting until you calculate the downside risk. Worrying is often worse than reality.

Please yourself first. Stop looking for acceptance and determine what YOU want out of life.

Control your fears. Don't worry about things that you can't control.

DECISIONS, DECISIONS, DECISIONS:

Difficult decisions made easy. Instead of laboring over a tough decision, determine the key decision-making criteria, and use these to evaluate your options. Then do it!

Be your own best friend. If you were giving advice to a good friend, what would you say? There's your answer.

Don't let your brain talk you out of it. Passion lives in the heart, not the head. So follow your heart, but don't forget to bring your brain.

Nothing is for life. Don't lose sleep if your decision doesn't pan out. Very few decisions are life altering, and there is almost always something to learn, as long as you try.

GO FOR IT:

Light small fires. Try something new. Start small. If it doesn't work out, limit your losses, and move on. If things go well, build on your successes.

Hit some singles. Some people set unrealistic expectations and overwhelm themselves in the process. Instead, set achievable, short-term goals while pursuing your long-term plans. Small wins will keep you motivated as you pursue your long-term goals.

Life doesn't go according to plan. Sometimes we create an "imaginary" plan and hold ourselves accountable to it. Be flexible. There's nothing wrong with deviating from the plan.

Break it down. When faced with a large problem, break it down into digestible parts. It's easier to address big problems in small pieces.

Don't quit. Never quit at the first sign of a challenge. Quitting is habit forming. But then again, so is winning.

Get going. Stop procrastinating and get started. Dreams, unlike eggs, don't hatch from sitting on them.

Dream BIG. Believe in the impossible. And then prove it CAN be done.

PURSUE YOUR PASSION TODAY

It doesn't matter what you're passionate about — what's important is being passionate about something that matters to you. So stop wishing and start doing; stop following and take the lead. It's time for you to stand up for your beliefs. It's time for you to make your opinions heard. It's time for you to make a difference in your life and in the lives of others around you. Get up from the couch and jump in with both feet. Sure . . . the road will be lined with caution signs, and there may even be some speed bumps along the way, but if you're positive and remain determined, you'll be happy that you tried. As Abraham Lincoln said, "And in the end, it's not the years in your life that count. It's the life in your years." So find your passion and pursue it today!

PASSION IS ABOUT
MORE THAN FINDING
YOUR CALLING IN LIFE.
IT MEANS CARING
INTENSELY ABOUT
WHO YOU ARE, WHAT
YOU STAND FOR,
AND WHAT YOU DO
EVERY DAY.

FRANK SONNENBERG

HONOR

TRUST ME . . . TRUST ME NOT

Trust is the fabric that binds us together, creating an orderly, civilized society from chaos and anarchy. If we can't trust our husband or our wife, if we can't trust our children, if we can't trust our boss or our colleagues, if we can't trust our preacher or our senator, then we have nothing on which to build a stable way of life. Trust is not an abstract, theoretical, idealistic goal forever beyond our reach. Trust — or a lack of it — is inherent in every action that we take and affects everything that we do. Trust is the cement that binds relationships, keeping spouses together, business deals intact, and political systems stable. Without trust, marriages fail, voters become apathetic, and organizations flounder.

Understanding the meaning of trust allows you to work toward being a trusted and trusting person. The truth is that trust is never guaranteed, and it can't be won overnight. Trust must be carefully constructed, vigorously nurtured, and constantly reinforced. Trust is established over time, gradually, through a long chain of successful experiences. In the early stages of relationships, whether personal or business, we extend ourselves in small ways and observe the responses to our actions. Then we take appropriate action, withdrawing, maintaining our behavior, or extending ourselves a bit further each time until trust is established. Although trust takes a long time to develop, it can be destroyed by a single action. Moreover, once lost, it is very difficult to re-establish.

THE FOUR STAGES OF TRUST

FIRST STAGE: FOUNDATION
History

Reputation

SECOND STAGE: SUPPORT STRUCTURE
The Values on Which Trust Rests

Integrity	Confidence	Reliability
Doing the right thing	Safety	Openness
Strength of conviction	Competence	Communication
	Fairness	

THIRD STAGE: CONSISTENCY

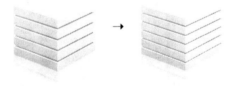

FOURTH STAGE: FROM PREDICTABILITY TO FAITH

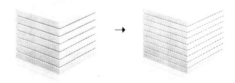

Building trusting relationships is a process that can best be described as stacking layers on a foundation one at a time in such a way that each layer bonds on top of the prior one before another layer is added.

FIRST STAGE: FOUNDATION

In a world where time is a precious resource, where we must often move without having the time to explore all the options, we use shortcuts to circumvent the process. For this reason, we develop first impressions about people. The most tangible form is a person's reputation. A reputation indicates how they might treat others both now and in the future.

SECOND STAGE: THE SUPPORT STRUCTURE

At the start of any relationship, people consciously or unconsciously examine actions rather than words to measure trustworthiness. As time goes by, the more that values such as integrity, fairness, and reliability are evident, the more people learn to trust one another and the stronger the relationship grows.

Integrity. There are a number of questions you ask yourself when assessing someone's integrity. Do they have a good value system? Do they avoid even the appearance of impropriety, and are they aware that the company they keep can be a reflection on their own integrity?

Doing the right thing. Another characteristic we look for when building relationships is whether people do the right thing not because they're afraid of being caught, but because it's the right thing to do.

Strength of conviction. Another set of questions to ask yourself when determining trustworthiness is: Do they stand up for what they believe in? Are they afraid to present their opinions?

Confidence. It is important to determine whether the people you build relationships with are comfortable enough to admit their faults and errors. Ask yourself: Do they always have to be right? Are they afraid to admit mistakes? If they cause a problem, do they try to fix it or do they look for people to blame?

Safety. When deciding whether to put your trust in someone, ask yourself whether they have a lot of emotional highs and lows. When conflicts arise, do they act in a caring and responsible fashion? Do they resolve problems and make decisions on the basis of logic, or do they make emotional judgments based on bias, residual anger, or desire to avenge the past?

Competence. Trust is increased when an individual is believed to be competent. An advanced degree, an affiliation with a well-respected organization, and professional status, all enhance the trustworthiness of an individual, but nothing is as useful as their actual performance.

Fairness. How much we trust people has a lot to do with our perception of their fairness. Are they objective? Do they show bias or favoritism? Do they present both sides of an issue or spin the issue to their advantage? Are they open-minded and willing to listen to new ideas?

Reliability. Another quality we look for when deciding whether or not to trust a person is reliability. We ask such questions as: Are they dependable? Do they follow through on promises made? If you ask for something, can you consider it done? Are they careful not to overstate what they will do?

Openness. Openness in relationships is built upon some existing level of trust. You feel comfortable confiding in people, knowing they would never breach your confidence or use the information against you at a later date. If they respond to that openness as expected, trust is enhanced and intimacy and honesty grow.

Communication. Communication is an essential quality in fostering trust. Lack of communication is particularly harmful when relevant information is withheld in order to maintain control or gain personal advantage.

Taken together, these qualities form the foundation on which trusting relationships are built. When they become part of a person's track record, relationships grow stronger and last longer.

THIRD STAGE: CONSISTENCY

Once people or organizations have repeatedly displayed traits mentioned above, we tend to increase our trust in them. We look for patterns that are regular and consistent because the more predictable people are, the higher the degree of comfort we have with them. In order to establish this, we ask ourselves whether we can anticipate actions.

FOURTH STAGE: FROM PREDICTABILITY TO FAITH

Now that consistency is established, we have a strong sense that we can predict what the person or the organization will do in the future. As a result, we do not question and worry about promises made: We trust them and are comfortable with our belief in them. This is the stage at which actions are so predictable that we don't consciously have to think about the relationship. At this phase, trust has become so integral a part of the relationship that we expect it to work. At their peak, relationships imbued with trust are bonded together by a faith so strong that it is very difficult to destroy the relationship. It is at this stage that people allow themselves to become entirely vulnerable to others.

FAIRNESS

FAIR
IS FAIR

T hey play favorites." "They made their mind up before they started."
"They didn't earn it." "They don't deserve it." "It's a popularity
contest." "They have more than me." And the list goes on and on. So
what's fair, and how is fairness determined?

Fairness affects everything we do. It shapes our judgment, impacts
our credibility, affects our ability to trust, and influences our loyalty and
motivation. It can bolster or damage a career, strengthen or torpedo a
relationship, and advance or ruin a leader's authority. In fact, fairness is so
important, it's a crucial element of a functioning democracy. And yet some
people complain that things aren't fair. Do some people get special
treatment? Are others rewarded without contributing? Do some folks
exploit the term "fairness" to get what they want? In any case, *if* these things
are happening, it's not fair.

WHAT MAKES A PERSON FAIR?

Rational. Fair-minded people employ clear and sensible thinking. They
examine both sides of an issue before forming an opinion. Fair-minded
people make decisions based on hard evidence and reason rather than
emotion; they know the whole story rather than just some of the facts.

Objective. Fair-minded people make impartial judgments, free from
personal bias. They disclose any bias before offering an opinion.

Open-minded. Fair-minded people are tolerant and non-discriminating,
accepting of the views of others. Fair-minded people are true to their own
beliefs without forcing them on others. As Oscar Wilde said, "Selfishness
is not living as one wishes to live, it is asking others to live as one wishes
to live."

Reasonable. Fair-minded people challenge others by setting high, yet realistic, expectations. They ask of others only what they're willing to do themselves. Furthermore, fair-minded people pay a fair day's wage for an honest day's work.

Even-handed. Fair-minded people give everyone an equal opportunity to succeed devoid of favoritism. They treat bosses and subordinates with the same level of respect. Furthermore, fair-minded people discourage any *real* or *perceived* favoritism that may result from conducting business with friends or acquaintances.

Sound judgment. Fair-minded people reward folks based on the value they provide rather than on the basis of subjective assessment.

Rule abiding. Fair-minded people follow the spirit as well as the letter of the law. They do what's right rather than what's politically expedient. Fair-minded people never twist rules for personal gain.

Contributor. Fair-minded people make a concerted effort to pull their own weight rather than living off the hard work of others. They "get in the game" rather than criticizing from the sidelines.

Deserving. Fair-minded people do not request special favors or accept unearned rewards. Furthermore, fair-minded people wait their turn in line rather than pushing their way to the front.

Sound leadership. Fair-minded people *earn* the respect of their colleagues through their expertise, personal integrity, and ability to foster trust rather than *demanding* it. When fair-minded people are in positions of power, they " do right" by people and go out of their way to serve as exemplary role models. Furthermore, fair-minded people create a win-win environment. They discourage situations in which people outmaneuver one another to gain the upper hand. They avoid zero-sum games in which one-person's win translates into another person's loss.

Selfless. Fair-minded people are empathetic, willing to walk in another person's shoes before making a judgment. Furthermore, as fair-minded people climb the ladder of success, they lift up others and are genuinely happy for their success.

SOMETIMES FAIRNESS IS A MATTER OF PERSPECTIVE

The characteristics of fairness aren't always clearly defined. In fact, they are a source of continual debate and can even be polarizing at times. You be the judge:

- Should exceptional performers be rewarded the same as underachievers?
- Should folks who work their butts off receive the same recognition as couch potatoes who watch?
- Should folks who assume significant risk in order to realize their dreams receive the same reward as those who pay lip service?
- Should some people be required to follow rules and others be given a pass?
- Should people who demand that others give of themselves be required to give equally of themselves?

Of course, ideologues believe that only *their* notion of fairness is correct. But is it fair for them to force their will on others? And so the debate continues . . .

LET'S BE FAIR

Fairness is about doing what's right. Period. Many people believe that being fair only affects others. The fact is, fairness — or the lack of it — says a lot about the giver even while it impacts the receiver. If we want to be effective and respected, it's essential that we behave fairly and provide an equal opportunity for others to succeed. Furthermore, in a civilized society, it is our responsibility to encourage others to do the same.

The truth is, everyone should have an equal opportunity to succeed, but then it is each individual's responsibility to capitalize on that opportunity. When equal opportunity is the norm, we are personally responsible for our destiny.

Hard work builds character, contributes to success, and promotes happiness. When we are rewarded for just showing up rather than for earning our way, it reduces confidence, promotes dependency, and robs us of our personal dignity. At the end of the day, it's our choice whether we're willing to make the commitment to succeed. As Andrew Carnegie said, "You cannot push anyone up the ladder unless he is willing to climb." Seems fair to me.

FORGIVENESS

FORGIVENESS: IT'S GOOD FOR YOU

We've all experienced some level of hurt and disappointment in our lives. It may have taken the form of a friend who betrayed us, a family member who disappointed us, a superior who exploited us, or an individual who caused some harm to our loved one. While some wounds are shallow and relatively easy to dismiss, others run deep, causing some to harbor anger or seek revenge. Others choose a second option . . . to forgive and forget.

Seeking retaliation, rather than forgiveness, traps you in the anger. In fact, some become so consumed by their bitterness that it harms them physically and mentally. The truth is, studies have found that forgiving is good for the body and the soul. As Buddha taught, "Holding on to anger is like grasping a hot coal with the intent of throwing it at someone else; you are the one who gets burned."

WHY IS FORGIVENESS SO HARD TO SWALLOW?

No one said that forgiving is easy. Here are some reasons why:

Revenge makes us feel better. The only way offenders can really know the hurt they inflicted is to experience it themselves. So we seek an eye for an eye.

Revenge will prohibit a repeat offense. While we can't undo what's already happened, we want to ensure that it isn't repeated. So we mount an aggressive campaign against the responsible party.

We desire justice. We're cynical that justice will be served. Therefore, the only way to "even the score" is through revenge.

We see no sign of remorse. We want closure. The problem is, the offender shows no sign of regret for the pain that he or she caused.

There is little chance of rehabilitation. We reason that some people are just bad apples with little prospect for change. We're concerned they'll receive leniency and repeat the offense.

It's difficult to let go of the anger. Some people cause so much anguish that we find it inconceivable to forgive them for the grief they caused.

The key is that forgiving doesn't mean forgetting, nor does it mean approving, what someone did. It just means that you're letting go of the anger toward that person.

THE POWER OF FORGIVENESS

There are several benefits to forgiveness. From a moral imperative, turning your cheek is the right thing to do. Period. Furthermore, it's a lot healthier and takes a lot less energy to forgive someone than to hold a grudge and remain angry. The fact is, when you're consumed by bitterness, resentment, and vengeance, you can get swallowed up by your anger. As Lewis B. Smedes, the renowned theologian, said, "To forgive is to set a prisoner free and discover that the prisoner was you."

Forgiveness does not mean suppressing your feelings or pretending the anger doesn't exist. Instead, forgiveness requires a conscious decision to release your resentment and thoughts of revenge. It also calls on you to acknowledge and practice the full range of emotions that you possess, such as grief and anger as well as kindness and compassion — even toward someone who has hurt you deeply.

That's tough, you say? It's important to remind yourself that one of the main reasons to show forgiveness is to benefit yourself. Hate is a cancer on one's soul. It can cause you to feel helpless and frustrated and trap you in a never-ending cycle of anger and resentment. And although you may have every reason to be bitter, you will be compounding the problem by keeping the issue alive. Think of it this way: While they hurt you once, now you're doing it to yourself.

The truth is, forgiveness reduces the offender's grip on you and helps you focus on other, positive areas of your life. So follow the wisdom of Robert Brault, the author, who said, "If you can't forgive and forget, pick one."

FORGIVING DOESN'T
MEAN FORGETTING,
NOR DOES IT MEAN
APPROVING, WHAT
SOMEONE DID. IT JUST
MEANS THAT YOU'RE
LETTING GO OF
THE ANGER TOWARD
THAT PERSON.

FRANK SONNENBERG

FAITH

BELIEVE

Some things are impossible, until they're not. BELIEVE!

Close your eyes and have a little faith in a power higher than yourself.
Things work out for no apparent reason.

When you least expect it, the stars will align, and magic will fill the air.
Your dreams will be born at the intersection of hope and reality.
You won't find an explanation for why,
because it may defy all logic and reason.

Remember that life unfolds in mysterious ways.
Yesterday you hoped for a miracle . . . today it became a reality.

When your miracle is born,
pinch yourself to make sure that it's real.
It doesn't matter why it happened.
The important thing is that it did.

If you're looking for the impossible to come your way, have a little faith.
Some of us don't believe in miracles, but for some of us, they occur every day.
It might as well be yours. BELIEVE!

Frank Sonnenberg

PERSPECTIVE

A NEW
DAY

Each day is a gift for you to carefully unwrap. What happens next is up to you. You can cherish every second that you're given or let time slip between your fingers. You can live every day with gusto and make every moment matter or you can be fearful and worry about what tomorrow will bring. You can reach out and make a difference in someone's life or focus on more ways to better your own. You can pursue new ways to grow as a person or wait to see if the world stops changing. You can reach for things that'll make you happy or you can be content with what you already have. You can drift along from dawn to dusk or live life like there's no tomorrow. . . . Before you know it, the seconds become minutes, the minutes become hours, and the day disappears into the night. Yesterday is a memory — a place you can visit only in your dreams. And remember, no matter how hard you try, you can never get your minutes back. Those minutes are gone forever.
Tomorrow is a new day.

Frank Sonnenberg

LIFE
LESSONS

YOUR HAPPINESS LIES IN THE BALANCE

D o you feel pulled in a million directions? I think we all feel that way. We're torn between wanting more and being satisfied with what we have . . . between choosing a fast-track career and having a "normal" family and social life . . . between taking another piece of chocolate and thinking about how we'll look in a bathing suit. Finding balance in life is a very noble pursuit, but it can be elusive and hard to achieve. How do you live a well-balanced life?

Because we're all unique, it's important to define what balance means to you and how you plan to achieve it. That process begins by establishing goals and determining priorities. Of course, there may be people who prefer to skip this step and cut to the chase, but if that path is taken, priorities will be chosen *for* them.

There are eight areas of our life that require careful balance. They are depicted in the following visual.

LIFE IS A BALANCING ACT

These are common dilemmas that we face each day. What's the right balance for you?

Having a fast-track career ●━━━●	Maintaining a vibrant family and social life
Making time to think ●━━━●	Completing a task
Eating what you love ●━━━●	Living a healthy lifestyle
Working for money ●━━━●	Doing what you love
Having "me" time ●━━━●	Being social with others
Spending money now ●━━━●	Saving for the future
Doing what you want ●━━━●	Doing what is expected of you
Spending time with the kids ●━━━●	Enjoying one-on-one time with your spouse
Pushing yourself to achieve more ●━━━●	Stopping to smell the roses
Trying something new ●━━━●	Overcoming fear of change
Advocating for your ideas ●━━━●	Compromising to gain acceptance
Responding to requests ●━━━●	Focusing on your priorities
Requesting help ●━━━●	Being self-sufficient
Following the crowd ●━━━●	Following your instinct
Holding people accountable ●━━━●	Forgiving and forgetting
Controlling the activity ●━━━●	Delegating responsibility
Waiting for someone ●━━━●	Moving on
Following your heart ●━━━●	Listening to your head

KEEPING LIFE IN BALANCE

Here are some guidelines for keeping your life in balance:

Remain focused and disciplined. Do you feel overwhelmed at times? That may be because you value quantity over quality. Priorities serve as guideposts to keep you on track. Your goal shouldn't be checking items off a to-do list, but rather doing things that matter.

Invest your time wisely. Resources are finite. When you overcommit your time or spread your resources too thin, you fail to dedicate the attention that your priorities deserve.

Learn to set boundaries. The goal shouldn't always be adding, but also subtracting from daily tasks. While any single request may seem reasonable, added together they'll divert your attention from your priorities. So learn to say "No." As Jessye Norman, award-winning opera singer and performer, said, "Problems arise in that one has to find a balance between what people need from you and what you need for yourself."

Minimize toxicity. While toxic food is bad for your health and well-being, so are negative and unethical people. They'll sap your energy and drain your soul.

Invest in relationships. Studies show that relationships are a key source of happiness. Being a good spouse, parent, or friend doesn't happen by chance. It requires an investment.

Try something new. Don't be so busy that you don't have time for something new. Expand your horizons. You won't know what the world offers unless you give it a try.

Treat yourself. Stop being so rigid by seeing the world as black or white. The fact is, most of life remains somewhere in between. So, if you're living at one end of the extreme, there's nothing wrong with deviating from your habit every once in a while.

Make time for nothing. Being busy doesn't always mean being productive. Set aside time to relax and think. It'll give you time to smell the roses and learn from each experience. It's important to enjoy the journey as well as the destination.

Be open to change. Love what you do and the choices that you make, but not so much that you're unwilling to change. There's a fine line between passion and obsession.

Live life with a purpose. Happiness isn't the result of accumulating things. It's about living life with a purpose.

Remember, it's not that you don't have enough time to devote to things that matter to you — but rather, the time needed was spent doing something else.

STRIKE THE RIGHT BALANCE

Many of us take each day as it comes and then seem surprised to find where life has taken us. We've risen to the top, but regret what we've lost during the journey; we've accumulated fancy possessions, but learned that money can't buy the best riches in life. It's as if we've followed a prepared script rather than consciously choosing the right path for us.

In the end, happiness is not a matter of intensity, but of balance. It's about thinking and doing; desiring more *and* being satisfied with what you have; doing what you want *and* what is expected of you. While this may sound simple, it's not easy. And it's not going to happen by itself. So determine what works best for you and be conscious of the choices that you make every day. As the saying goes, "The key to keeping your balance is knowing when you've lost it." Your happiness lies in the balance.

REPUTATION: YOU CAN'T RUN FROM YOUR SHADOW

In a world where time is a precious resource, we often draw conclusions without examining all the information that's available to us. We rely on shortcuts, such as someone's reputation, to simplify the process. Did the job applicant have a good reference? What did my neighbor say about the contractor? How was the restaurant review? In short, we place tremendous value on credible sources to help us make decisions every day.

WHAT ARE PEOPLE SAYING ABOUT YOU?

Your reputation is like a shadow, following you wherever you go. You can't disguise it, you can't hide from it, and you certainly can't run from it. It will follow you for life. And although it's said that you can't be in two places at the same time, you actually do it every day — your reputation serves as your stand-in whenever you're not around.

Your reputation can be your best friend or worst enemy. It can open doors to marvelous opportunities or ensure that every door is slammed right in your face. What does your reputation say about you? Does your "shadow" promote you as an upstanding individual or drag you through the mud?

A moving target. Your reputation is constantly evolving. Over time, the cumulative observations of your words AND actions form the basis of your reputation. And it's not only what you do but also how others perceive your motives that often counts most.

Your reputation can be influenced by such behavior as:

- Was your joke at the office party in bad taste?
- How did you treat the employee after the infraction?
- Was your Facebook post inappropriate?
- Were you tactful in lodging the complaint?
- Do you get along with your peers?
- Did you help your colleague when he or she was in a pinch?
- How do you treat your pet?
- Are you a fair-weather friend?
- Do you play office politics?
- Can you keep a secret?
- Are you a team player or merely out for yourself?
- How do you react under pressure?
- Were you gracious in accepting the award?
- Do you accept responsibility for your actions?

What do you stand for? Your reputation is much too valuable to treat casually. But if *you* don't know what you stand for, you're leaving it all to chance. Take 10 minutes to get to know the real you. When you look in the mirror every morning, are you happy with what you see? How would you define your values and core principles? What matters most to you in life? Are you the kind of friend that you'd want as a friend? How would you define the "*ideal* you" compared to the real you? If you were tasked with writing your obituary today, what three things best describe you? If you don't like what you see, don't blame the mirror.

Consistency is key. When your behavior is steady and reliable, your actions become predictable. This enables people to form an impression of you and anticipate future behavior. As time goes on, any deviation from your normal behavior is characterized as an anomaly or that you're having "a bad day." On the other hand, if your behavior is erratic and unpredictable, you're sending mixed messages and leaving your reputation open to confusion and misinterpretation.

There's no excuse. While it takes significant time and effort to build a solid reputation, you can destroy your standing in the blink of an eye. A flaming email, a sarcastic remark, a neglected "thank you," or a missed commitment is all it takes. For the most part, people are very forgiving if you make an honest mistake or act out of character on occasion. But when improper actions — such as lying, cheating, or stealing — are repeated or *intentional*, however, your reputation suffers. Even if you offer a heartfelt apology after a transgression, it can still take considerable time and effort to recover.

News travels fast. In years past, reputations were formed primarily through word of mouth — and that continues to remain true today. The difference is that we've migrated from one-on-one conversations to social media (such as Facebook, Twitter, Google+, and LinkedIn), which spread news to thousands of people around the world at the click of a mouse. Furthermore, the Internet makes news permanent. Once bad news starts to snowball downhill, it can take a Herculean effort to slow the momentum. For that reason, nasty rumors and gossip must be addressed head-on before irreparable damage takes place.

Rome wasn't built in a day. Many people ask if a tarnished reputation can be repaired. The quick answer is yes, BUT don't expect to achieve success overnight. A tarnished reputation takes time and complete honesty to repair. The only way to mend your reputation is by rebuilding trust in small increments. Baby steps help others connect the dots and build bridges between your actions. On the other hand, *aggressively* trying to change your reputation often ends up doing more harm than good. Significant, "overnight" changes in behavior can defy credibility and cause others to be more suspicious than trustful of the "new you."

YOUR REPUTATION SHADOWS YOU EVERYWHERE

Protect your reputation like it's the most valuable asset you own. Because it is! You can't escape your shadow, but you *can* shape your reputation. Here are seven actions that you can take to build and defend your reputation:

1. **Values matter.** Operate with integrity at all times. Do what's right. Period. That way, you'll never have to look over your shoulder to see who's watching.

2. **Stand for something.** People crave consistency and predictability. Maintain the strength of your ideas and principles.

3. **Take pride in what you do.** If you're not proud of what you're doing, either you're not finished yet, or the effort is not worthy of your best self.

4. **Accept responsibility for your actions.** If you wouldn't be proud to see your words or actions in a headline, don't say or do them. If things go wrong despite your best intentions, don't hide. Face the music with an apology and your plan to improve.

5. **Think before you act.** Count to 10 before losing your temper, sending a flaming email, or making a caustic remark — or you may live to regret it.

6. **Be a good-reputation ambassador.** Help others build and sustain their reputations by acknowledging their good works, by modeling good behaviors yourself, and by never engaging in reputation assassination.

7. **Let your conscience be your guide.** Your character matters most when no one is looking.

People love their toys. They safeguard their precious cell phones, cars, and computers, even though they're replaced every few years. On the other hand, your reputation is uniquely yours and remains with you for life. Sometimes it even stands in for you in your absence. The fact is, every time you make a move, your shadow (or reputation) moves along with you. Make it reflect well on you. You can't run from your shadow.

PROTECT YOUR
REPUTATION
LIKE IT'S THE MOST
VALUABLE ASSET
YOU OWN.
BECAUSE IT IS!

FRANK SONNENBERG

WHAT DO TOUGH TIMES SAY ABOUT YOU?

It's one thing to have a bad day yet quite another to fall on tough times. These are the days when it's hard to get out of bed, not knowing how you're going to make it through the day. These are the days when it feels like the world is crumbling around you and you've been hit by a two-by-four by the time you go to bed at night. Yet, these are the times that shape character and show what you're made of. So what do tough times say about you?

Unfortunately, for most of us there comes a time when we will experience a major setback. Whether we're confronted by a personal tragedy, faced with a serious financial crisis, or struck by an uncontrollable event, these are the times that test our will and our spirit.

Everyone reacts to these situations differently. Some people get angry, feel sorry for themselves, and cast blame; other people remain calm, create an action plan to move forward, and look for a trace of blue in the dark skies ahead. The fact is, the way you respond to these situations in the short term can impact your *long-term* success and happiness. As George S. Patton said, "The test of success is not what you do when you are on top. Success is how high you bounce when you hit bottom."

CHARACTER MATTERS DURING TOUGH TIMES

Be positive. Surround yourself with positive and supportive people.

Remain calm and levelheaded. Count to ten. Try to make decisions based on fact rather than emotion.

Accept support. There are wonderful people who care about you. Don't shut them out, or worse, take your problem out on them. They're trying to help.

Learn from the past. Have you faced a similar situation in the past? Apply lessons learned. There's no need to reinvent the wheel.

Seek professional counsel. Identify someone to serve as a sounding board. Gain from their knowledge, experience, and objective viewpoint.

Face reality. Don't run away from the problem; run toward it. Accept reality as it is, not as you want it to be.

Own the problem. Don't waste precious time and energy making excuses or casting blame. Move forward rather than dwelling in the past.

Make tough choices. Don't procrastinate or hold out for the perfect answer; there may not be one. Identify your options and create a plan of action. You'll gain more from moving forward in a deliberate fashion than from running around like a chicken without a head.

Set priorities. Don't treat every option or activity equally. It's smarter to do the important things rather than to complete every item on your list.

Build momentum. Big problems are best solved in small pieces. Tackle short-term items to achieve wins while you address the root cause.

Remain true to your values. This is no time to compromise your integrity. Listen to your conscience. You have to live with yourself for the rest of your life.

Be loyal. Don't throw anyone under the bus to save your hide. In fact, putting the needs of others first may supply the positive energy you need to move forward.

Find an outlet for relaxation. Life is a marathon, not a sprint. Identify ways to relax and reduce stress. That'll help you complete the mission with your sanity intact.

Be a leader. These are the times when real leaders show their character. Lead by example. Be the first to "take a hit" before asking others to do the same.

Never quit. As Richard M. Nixon said, "A man is not finished when he's defeated. He's finished when he quits."

Keep the faith. When nothing seems to work, faith often does.

Learn from the experience. Make sure to learn from the experience. You may have to apply this lesson another day. One thing this teaches us is that life is filled with "ups and downs," so make the most of the "in-betweens."

FROM TOUGH TIMES TO GOOD TIMES

Believe in yourself. This too shall pass. This isn't the first or the last time that you're going to face tough times. If the situation is within your control, do something about it; if not, accept it for what it is and try to make the best of it. You survived the last time you faced a crisis, and you will this time as well. Remember, it's not going to get better by sitting around. In fact, left unattended, small problems often become bigger ones.

It's easy to look like a star when times are good, but when times are tough, your true character comes into full view. Be strong. Don't compromise your integrity; don't lower your standards; and above all, don't quit. You're better than that. You owe it to yourself to overcome the problem, as you have so many times before. There is great wisdom in Friedrich Nietzsche's truism, "That which does not kill us makes us stronger." The key is to get through tough times with dignity and grace. So hold your head up high. No one ever said it's easy. And for that, you'll have more reason to be proud when it's over. Tough times say a lot about us. Let's hope that they say only good things about you!

BLUFFING YOUR WAY TO THE TOP

Remember the days when you were in school, and you studied your tail off for an exam? You celebrated when you received your grade only to find out that one of your classmates, who had partied the night before, blew the socks off the exam because he had gotten a hold of the test questions beforehand.

You thought that after you graduated, you had left all that baggage behind. Then you find out that these same characters are soaring through the corporate ranks because — you guessed it — they've learned how to "play the system."

Well, I've got a message for these counterfeit superstars: If you think you can bluff your way through life, you've got something coming.

Eventually, people see right through these shortcuts to success. In fact, these counterfeit superstars are living on borrowed time. The day will come when their ways will come back to bite them. GOTCHA!

Despite the fact that the majority of people play by the rules and try to do the right thing, there are a number of bad actors in every organization who have no problem advancing their careers on the backs of others. Here are some you may recognize:

Emperors. These people climb the corporate ladder by capitalizing on who they know and where they've been, rather than on what they're contributing today. They may have friends in high places, have their walls filled with diplomas, or have previously worked for a blue-chip company. They're like an oasis. They may look wonderful from a distance, but the closer you get, the more obvious it becomes that it's all just a mirage. In this case, emperors truly have no clothes.

Pretty Boys (or Girls). These people really look the part. They are the trendiest dressers, belong to the finest country clubs, and look like they could be on the cover of Vogue or GQ. Similar to Emperors, the Pretty set rise up the corporate ladder based on appearance rather than performance. But their veneer is thin, and when the spotlight gets too bright, you can begin to see right through them. In this case, you shouldn't judge a book simply by its cover.

A-- Kissers. These people spend all their time fawning over their superiors. You need to reduce costs? No problem. We just won't give people raises this year. (Too bad there's only enough for management.) These A-- Kissers spend 99.9 percent of their time in closed-door management meetings with little time to provide direction for their own team — regardless of the impact that it has on results. In this case, it's only a matter of time before their people say "ENOUGH!" and tell THEM to kiss off.

Delegators. They say there are only two kinds of people, those who are willing to work and those who are willing to let them. These counterfeit superstars are in the latter group. They have the power to say: "You want something done? No problem. In fact, rather than get it to you by Friday, how about tomorrow morning?" Then they get their staff to stay late while they walk out the door at 5 p.m. These people always volunteer for more work; are calm, cool, and collected; and have the cleanest desks in the office. How is that possible? It's because they delegate everything! In this case, the only thing that stops at their desk is the credit they don't deserve, not the work.

Schmoozers. These folks could win an award for Mr. or Ms. Congeniality. Everybody loves them. Schmoozers know all the ballgame stats; they know how to tell a joke; and they're up-to-date on the inside dirt. Their colleagues like them so much that they don't mind taking on their workload while the schmoozer is entertaining clients elsewhere. In this case, work is a party for schmoozers.

Bystanders. These slouches do just enough to get by. They've been with the organization for a zillion years, rarely speak up, never make waves, and would make themselves invisible if they could. They spend their day moving piles of paper on their desk while they watch everyone else go crazy trying to get the job done. In fact, when they're out on vacation, nobody even knows they're missing. In this case, the last survivors on Earth, along with cockroaches, will be the bystanders.

Scavengers. These are the types who take the credit for everybody else's work. They surround themselves with wonderful, talented people and spend the day determining if there's an idea worth stealing and fine-tuning their personal PR machine. In this case, they'll continue to rise up the company ranks as long as their "credit" remains good.

Busybodies. These individuals spend their whole day trying to prove how busy they are — rather than getting anything done. Whenever they're asked to do something, they spend twenty minutes describing how much work they have on their plate. In this case, if busybodies ever needed a role model, they could look to a turnstile — it's out in front, goes around in circles, creates wind, but never gets anywhere.

Any of these personality types sound familiar? Don't get angry if you know some of these people — they'll get their due. They think they're fooling the world, but, sooner or later, everyone catches on to them.

Chances are they started pulling small stunts when they were young and then refined their game over time. Why? Because they've had to . . . they're not competitive in a fair contest and the only way they feel they can win is by bending the rules in their own direction.

The fact is, by pulling their antics, these counterfeit superstars not only make colleagues row harder to compensate for their deficiencies, they steal the spotlight from very talented people who deserve the recognition. This destroys morale, hurts productivity, and damages competitiveness.

Sounds a bit bleak for the HONEST-DAY'S-WORK folks, doesn't it? Don't give up. And for goodness' sake, don't feel that you have to become one of them to succeed.

As time goes on, you'll be able to look back on a life distinguished by integrity and self-respect. Meanwhile, these counterfeit superstars will start believing their own press, and they'll get sloppy. Or they'll go over the edge due to the pressure of their own duplicity. Or — ultimately — if they're not caught, they'll meet their match when they run into someone else who beats them at their own game. GOTCHA!

MY KID
THE
SUPERSTAR

As parents, we think the world of our kids. So, when they possess a particular talent, "naturally" we think they're ready for the Olympics, a run on Broadway, or a college scholarship.

At games, you'll find some proud parents cheering their children for giving it their best shot, while others "browbeat" their kids — sometimes pushing them to their physical and emotional limits — and frequently, just harassing or embarrassing them in front of their friends. It's no wonder that many kids lose interest in an activity because it's no longer rewarding and fun. It makes you wonder whether winning means more to the parents or to their children.

Whatever happened to simply enjoying an activity? When did we turn Pee Wee sports into killer competition? Since when did we place more emphasis on "winning" than on building confidence and self-respect? Sure . . . some kids will translate their talent into stardom and a professional career. As for the others . . . these activities can provide a wonderful learning experience about life — *if* we would just treat them that way — while "letting our kids be kids."

WHAT SHOULD ACTIVITIES TEACH OUR KIDS ABOUT LIFE?

Attitude is everything. Be positive. Set high expectations. Picture yourself a winner. Replace negative thinking with a can-do attitude.

Get in the game. Anyone can watch a game, but real winners get off the sidelines and play. Don't let fear of failure stop you from reaching your full potential. Remember, it's better to go down swinging than to be called out on strikes.

Winning is as much mental as physical. Surround yourself with positive people. Control your emotions. Stay focused and remain disciplined.

Master the fundamentals. Practice, practice, practice. When you master the basics, and execute them well, there's no need to worry about the score. It works like magic.

Few things come easy in life. Success is achieved through hard work and determination. If you want something, you have to put your heart into it. It takes many years to become an overnight success.

Always do your best. Aim high and never settle for second best. Strive for continuous improvement in everything that you do. As Vince Lombardi once said, "Winning is not everything — but making the effort to win is." If you try your best, you'll never have regrets.

Be ready on game day. Anyone can talk a good game. What matters is what you do when it counts. There's no dress rehearsal for life.

Remain flexible and embrace change. You can't control the uncontrollable. So be prepared to expect the unexpected. People get injured. The weather doesn't always cooperate. The ball won't always come your way. Go with the flow.

View obstacles as opportunities. When barriers get in your way, find a way around them and use them to learn and develop. Don't feel sorry for yourself. Excuses don't win games.

Know your strengths and the strengths of others. You're only one person, so don't try to win games by yourself. Trust and support your teammates and they'll place their faith in you. That's the making of a winning team.

Be a team player. Winning takes teamwork. So be prepared to make personal sacrifices for the good of the team.

Keep your perspective. Remain calm under pressure. Competition will test your limits. Be calm, strong, and in control when it matters most. When counting to ten doesn't seem to work, try twenty.

Be a leader. Become a good role model. Set high standards of excellence for yourself and others. Make people feel special and help bring out the best in everyone. Now that's a superstar.

If you can't play fair, don't play. Integrity matters. Compete fairly and fully. When you resort to cheating, you've already lost.

Quitting is not an option. There will be times when things get tough — and it may even feel as though all is lost. Always keep hope alive and display confidence in the eye of defeat. As Morgan Freeman said, "The best way to guarantee a loss is to quit."

Accept responsibility for your actions. You're in the driver's seat. Only you can decide how hard you're willing to work to achieve your goals. If you succeed, the rewards are yours. If you fail, there's always another day.

Learn to forgive. Be loyal when the chips are down. Appreciate the special qualities of others, including your opponents. Forgive the mistakes of others. It may be your error that costs the team tomorrow.

Support others in need. Real friends are available in good times and bad. So offer your teammates encouragement and support, especially when they have a bad day.

Look to the future rather than the past. Don't dwell on mistakes or past defeats. What's done is done. Learn from the experience and move on.

Follow directions. Listen to your coach and respect the call of a referee even if you disagree.

Compete against yourself. Competing against others may be destructive if more effort is spent tearing others down than building yourself up. When you compete against yourself, however, you both win.

Raise your game. Find a good role model. Don't be shy to ask for help. Be open to feedback and put it to good use.

Say "no" to unhealthy behavior. Take care of your body. It's the only one you've got. Abuse your body and pay the price.

Know that losing doesn't make you a failure. Be a good loser. Bounce back after a big loss. That's the sign of a superstar.

Be a good winner. Be a winner on and off the field. Be humble and quietly proud but never self-satisfied. And never let success go to your head.

PREPARING KIDS FOR THE GAME OF LIFE

Teach your child that success doesn't come easily. Life is a continuing competition in which excellence wins. Therefore, it's better to learn how to compete when the consequences are small. So if you aren't using every opportunity to prepare your child for the game of life, your son or daughter is being cheated out of something very special.

Take your cue from the great coaches in all sports and at all levels — great coaches build trust, instill discipline, and foster teamwork. They showcase the child who displays a can-do attitude, shows improvement, or demonstrates leadership on and off the field. Great coaches inspire confidence by applauding the team because they did their best — even if they lost the game.

The bottom line is that kids aren't born with self-confidence or a positive attitude; kids don't automatically know how to conquer fear, accept feedback, overcome obstacles, or snatch victory from the jaws of defeat; kids don't always know what it's like to come back after failure, be a humble winner, or show grace after a terrible loss. These skills are learned.

As Mike Krzyzewski, the legendary Duke basketball coach, said, "My ambition in high school was to be a high school coach and teacher, and that's still what I do: teach." So do your child a favor and teach him or her the winning philosophy of great coaches — because even though it's great to win the game, it's even better to be a superstar in life.

LIFE IS A CONTINUING
COMPETITION IN
WHICH EXCELLENCE
WINS. THEREFORE,
IT'S BETTER TO LEARN
HOW TO COMPETE
WHEN THE
CONSEQUENCES
ARE SMALL.

FRANK SONNENBERG

HOW HEAVY
IS YOUR
BAGGAGE?

I magine carrying a backpack filled with rocks everywhere you go. Now that's exhausting! It gives new meaning to the phrase "doing the heavy lifting."

If the weight of that backpack seems like too much to bear, just imagine the impact of the emotional baggage that we carry every day! Think about it . . . we *fear* getting fired, we *complain* about the service we receive, we *express disgust* over government politics, we envy the person "next door," we *worry* about meeting deadlines, and we *discredit* our colleague for "stealing" the promotion. Emotional baggage? You bet.

Now ask yourself: What do we gain by gossiping about a colleague, bad-mouthing politicians, or ranting about our frustrations on Facebook? The truth is, besides being a colossal waste of time, nothing really changes — except that we're not much fun to be around. Who needs that?

Even when we don't overtly express our negative feelings of worry, preju-dice, fear, criticism, guilt, anger, and envy, we play out these "dramas" in our heads like a chess master plotting his next few moves. These negative thoughts race through our minds like a whirlwind, making us more and more anxious each time we revisit them. In fact, some people get so overwhelmed and depressed that they worry themselves into a frenzy, making it tough to concentrate during the day and causing sleep issues at night. Taken to the extreme, emotional baggage can be absolutely debilitating if not controlled.

In days gone by in a labor-intensive society, hard work resulted in tired bones and sore muscles. In the Information Age, our bodies tell us that enough is enough by reacting with stress-related ailments ranging from headaches to backaches to anxiety attacks. And over time, these stresses add up.

The bottom line is that these "emotional tirades" are unproductive, unhealthy, and exhausting. They cause us to lose focus, snap at people we care about, and waste precious time playing these ridiculous mind games. No wonder we're exhausted.

TAKE A LOAD OFF YOUR MIND

Here are some simple suggestions to reduce your emotional baggage masquerading as worry, prejudice, fear, criticism, guilt, anger, and envy.

Food for thought. One of the first steps that people take when trying to lose weight is writing down the food they eat each day. It's surprising to see it in writing and represents an important motivator toward changing eating habits. By listing the negative thoughts that cross our minds each day, we can use the same technique to reduce our emotional baggage.

Keep it positive. Negative thinking isn't always bad. In fact, having some fear and worry keeps you on your toes, forces you to prepare *early*, and encourages you to anticipate future events by asking yourself, what if? That's positive. On the other hand, when emotional baggage makes you angry, increases your anxiety, or overwhelms you, it's a negative to avoid.

Is that a fact? It's very helpful to determine if the assumptions behind your fears, worries, prejudices, etc., are factual and realistic. When you're tired, emotional, or under stress, negative thoughts can spiral out of control and ruin your day, even if the premise behind your anxiety is far-fetched. That's a fact.

The sky is falling! How often do your fears and worries actually come true? If they rarely come to fruition, why are you getting all worked up? Odds are that you'd have a better chance of getting hit by lightning.

Make it happen. Many situations involve matters beyond our control. If you can't affect the outcome, you may as well enjoy your day — because even a Herculean effort won't make a difference. Therefore, if there's a problem that's waking you up at 3 a.m., and you can do something to make it better, even at that hour, *do it*. If not, it's better to *forgetaboutit* and deal with it in the morning. And if it's truly beyond your control, then all your worry and sleeplessness won't change the situation. It's time to put the worry behind you and move on.

Will it even matter? Some situations appear larger than life, yet in hindsight seem inconsequential. The key is to gauge the issue beforehand. As a simple test, ask yourself whether you'll remember the problem in a year or two. If not, it may be a trivial issue unworthy of your concern.

BREAK FREE FROM YOUR BAGGAGE

It's unfair to assume that it's easy to unpack the emotional baggage that we've accumulated over a lifetime. If Buddha's words are true, "What we think, we become," then it's vital to take control of our lives. But let's be realistic.

The anxiety that *we* create in our minds is often worse than reality. We worry about impressing our friends, when the truth is that *real* friends remain good friends in good times and bad. We worry about being late for a meeting. If we are, it won't change mankind. We also get angry waiting home all day for a delivery person. And that too shall pass. Again, Buddha said it well, "Holding on to anger is like grasping a hot coal with the intent of throwing it at someone else; you are the one getting burned."

The truth is, in most cases, life goes on. You have the power to make yourself happy or miserable during your life journey. There are very few times in life when we hit a wall so hard that we don't recover from it. We pick ourselves up, dust ourselves off, and move on. The difference is, if you take a pledge to be positive, and start reducing your emotional baggage, you're going to lead a happier, healthier, more fulfilling life. As Norman Vincent Peale once said, "Change your thoughts and you change your world."

THE HAVES
AND
HAVE-NOTS

Some people have an "unfair advantage" in the marathon race called life. This advantage will enable them to climb the ladder quickly and enjoy all the benefits that success offers. You may be thinking that these lucky folks won't earn their achievements; that they were born with a silver spoon in their mouth and are being given assistance that only a few receive. Welcome to the world of the haves and have-nots.

The fact is, the "unfair advantage" that will give these folks their head start can be found in the strong *foundation* they are receiving: nurturing parents or caregivers, access to a good education, wonderful role models to emulate, and an upbringing that embraces good values. Everything they achieve later in life will build on this foundation and is earned through their own hard work and effort.

Although some may think that money can *buy* a good foundation, nothing could be further from the truth — it requires love and dedication. The fact is, a good education isn't solely the responsibility of a teacher . . . it requires a partnership between the school and the family. Setting a good example doesn't happen overnight . . . it requires a commitment to be a good role model day in and day out. Good values aren't learned by magic . . . they require consistent reinforcement and commitment. *These aren't gifts of the wealthy, but of the caring.*

A FOUNDATION FOR SUCCESS DOESN'T HAPPEN BY CHANCE

Providing a good foundation is easier said than done. After an exhausting day at work, it's easier to stare at the TV than review your child's homework; when your kid does something wrong, it's easier to let it slide than to be the "bad guy" and discipline him or her; when your kid is surrounded by bad influences, it's easier to look the other way, than to confront the issue head-on; and when your child meets defeat, it's easier to "blame the world" rather than help your child accept responsibility and learn from the setback.

The difference between the haves and have-nots is dependent on the foundation that we provide our kids. Here's what it takes:

Nurturing. Parenting is not a part-time job. Children require continual encouragement and support. Parents are the cheerleaders who provide hope and optimism for the future.

Personal sacrifice. Parents are selfless people willing to forgo a great deal to benefit their children. They dream of offering their children a better life than they had.

Discipline. Parents know that disciplining a child is not easy. Although it's rarely appreciated, it's often in the child's best interest.

Personal responsibility. Parents know that it takes a village to raise a child, but they do not outsource responsibility for building a good foundation for their kids. They also teach their children to accept responsibility for their actions and choices.

Empathy. Parents teach kids that success is the result of hard work. And although occasional disappointment is inevitable, they shouldn't let it derail the journey. Parents are always there to provide a ray of sunshine when the sky fills with clouds.

Inner voice. When kids grow up, they hear their parent's voice in their subconscious. Make sure the words they hear offer positive messages.

Setting an example. Parents know their behavior will be emulated. Therefore, they can instill good personal values and a strong work ethic by serving as exemplary role models. Furthermore, they know that friends and family, teachers and pastors, celebrities and athletes, and even video games, movies, and music influence behavior. Are they a good or bad influence?

Family. The family provides a child with roots, much-needed structure, and unconditional love. Families also provide their children with a happy home —a place where a child is always safe and welcome.

THE MOST REWARDING EXPERIENCE OF A LIFETIME

It's hard for parents to measure the result of their hard work in weeks, months, or even years. But one day your children will grow up and you'll see that your efforts paid off. You'll take great pride in knowing that you raised well-adjusted kids. They're honest and ethical, ambitious and self-reliant, hardworking and disciplined, compassionate and modest. They have strong moral character, impeccable values, and a sense of purpose. They're going to go places in life, and you played a pivotal role in building their foundation for success.

Although you won't see fireworks lighting the sky, there's nothing more gratifying than seeing what you've accomplished. As Franklin D. Roosevelt said, "We may not be able to prepare the future for our children, but we can at least prepare our children for the future." That's what parenting is all about, isn't it? Your parents did it for you, and your children will do the same thing for their children. Some people ask what success is . . . well now you know. You raised great kids. And because of your love and dedication, they have a bright future ahead of them. Yes . . . there is a difference between the haves and have-nots. Because of you, your kids have it all.

THE
CHOICE
IS YOURS

We're all confronted by countless choices each day. Some have minimal consequences, such as whether to have our ice cream in a cup or cone, while other decisions can be life changing. And while some of these choices may impact our lives today, other choices may not affect us for years to come.

We are a product of the choices we make. Each decision helps to define who we are and how we're different from one another.

Unfortunately, some folks prefer to make their decisions in a haphazard fashion. They "shoot from the hip" or flip a coin rather than reviewing their options in a deliberate manner. Others simply follow the crowd rather than base their decisions on an idea's true merits. Lastly, some people are more interested in checking an item off their to-do list than in making a sound choice. In this case, expediency trumps effectiveness. Of course, not every decision requires in-depth analysis. But poor choices do have their consequences, and being fully engaged in the decision process is a good practice in itself.

IT'S YOUR CHOICE: VALUES MATTER

Personal values should serve as your guiding star in making good choices. Values are like a pilot's flight plan . . . without them you're flying blind. Unfortunately, some people don't take the time to define them.

Take a moment and consider the following items. Your response doesn't have to be limited to either extreme and there's no correct answer to each question. In fact the right answer is the one that's best for *you*.

Life balance: Do you put more effort into building your career or spending time with friends and family?

Self-satisfaction: Do you spend more time trying to please yourself or to satisfy others?

Risk: Are you risk averse or would you gamble to win big?

Commitments: Are you more apt to make serious commitments or to live a happy-go-lucky life?

Wants–needs: Do you spend more time enjoying what you have or upgrading your belongings?

Opportunity: Are you content with your existing situation or willing to explore exciting new opportunities?

Healthy living: Are you more inclined to follow a healthy diet or to yield to temptation?

Trust: Do you put trust and faith in other people or rely mostly upon yourself?

Work ethic: Are you willing to pay your dues as an investment in your future, or do you prefer to take it easy and possibly limit your opportunities?

Relationships: Do you put more effort into developing deep relationships or casual friendships?

Saving: Are you more inclined to save for a rainy day or to shop till you drop?

Personal growth: Do you invest time in self-development, or are you comfortable where you are in life?

Purpose: Do you measure success by what you give to others or by how much you've personally gained?

The preceding list isn't intended to be exhaustive. Its purpose is to help you define who you are and what you stand for. One of the realities is that every choice you make has both a benefit and a cost. For example, saving versus spending. People who fail to save for a rainy day may enjoy the satisfaction that comes with their new acquisitions, but they wind up disappointed when unforeseen expenses blindside them. On the other hand, folks who save too much may be depriving themselves and their loved ones of things that they truly need.

IT'S YOUR CHOICE: TAKE CHARGE

Making good choices begins with taking charge of the decision-making process.

Manage the big stuff. It's very easy to get sidetracked by insignificant issues in life. If you spend a lot of time on trivial stuff, you won't have time to contemplate things that matter.

Values matter. As we've noted, make decisions that are consistent with your core beliefs and values. The alternative invariably leads to regret.

Learn from the past. Learn from your experiences and the experiences of others. Identify situations where you've had a similar choice in the past. How can you apply those lessons learned to the existing situation?

Know what you know and what you don't know. Don't try to be an expert in everything. Seek input and advice when variables lie outside your comfort zone.

Keep the right perspective. View an issue from every vantage point. What do the facts say? What is your intuition telling you? Is your conscience trying to tell you something? Listen up.

Don't procrastinate. You'll rarely have all the information that you need to make a "perfect" decision. So don't demand perfection. As Voltaire once said, "The perfect is the enemy of the good."

Once you make a decision, don't look back, make it work. Don't second-guess yourself. You can't relive the past. It's a waste of valuable time and energy.

IT'S YOUR CHOICE: DEFINE SUCCESS IN YOUR OWN TERMS

Life's not about checking an item off your to-do list or trying to impress others with how busy you are. Life's about being content with where you've been, where you are now, and where you're going. It's about being proud of who you are, what you represent, and the impact that you're having on others. This begins and ends with the choices that you make. So give some serious thought to every choice you face. As Albert Camus once said, "Life is a sum of all your choices." Are you happy with the path that you're choosing for yourself? The choice is yours.

LIVING
LIFE ON
THE EDGE

Some people live life on the edge every day and love every minute of it. They get a rush by taking on seemingly insurmountable challenges and beating the odds. The fact is, engaging in risky behavior is no different from gambling. Whether you bet the ranch on a get-rich-quick scheme, buy too much stuff on credit, or ignore your doctor's warnings — the result is the same — a willingness to risk it all. If your luck runs out, the downside can be devastating, resulting in failed relationships, financial hardship, or even death. Why do it?

WHAT DO YOU HAVE TO LOSE?

Let's look at some bets that are placed every day:

Getting rich quick. There'll always be get-rich-quick schemes and the people to fund them. Remember Phineas Taylor Barnum? While there is some dispute about the famous quote associated with his name, there is little doubt that gullibility and greed don't make for effective investment strategies. For those who think that landing the BIG ONE is only a matter of time, the prospect of losing just isn't in the cards. Whether it's the next gold rush, dot-com investing, or flipping homes, these greedy folks try their luck in the hope of "winning the lottery." Unfortunately, most of these schemes end the same way . . . disappointment, indebtedness, or worse. Like musical chairs, if you can't find a chair when the music stops playing, you're out of the game. In the game of life, you're also out of luck. Unfortunately, there's no way to make a quick buck without some risk. If there were, most everyone would be wealthy.

Living large. Some people, like sharks, spend their entire life hunting and consuming. All the oceans in the world can't satisfy these eating machines. When the sharks can't afford their buying addiction, they purchase their "toys" on credit. The problem is, if they're not careful, they'll be making hefty monthly payments without receiving anything tangible in return. Whatever happened to living within your means, much less saving money for a rainy day?

Betting the ranch. Whoa, partner! People who try to increase their personal wealth without protecting their existing assets may be betting the ranch. If you don't guard against downside risk, it's a cinch that you're leaving yourself vulnerable to substantial loss and may not even know it. Just think about those entrepreneurs who fail to protect their businesses through a limited liability company or incorporation. They may wind up sacrificing all their personal assets if they happen to get sued and lose in court. A similar example comes from one of the biggest causes of personal bankruptcy: the onset of serious illness without adequate health insurance coverage. And if that happens, there goes the ranch, and that's no bull.

Taking care of business. How many times do people receive advice to drop five pounds, stop smoking, exercise thirty minutes each day, or lay off the fried foods? Sometimes this advice is suggested as a preventive measure. Other times, it's given to someone rehabilitating from a serious illness. Why take the chance? If you don't listen to the experts' advice, there may be more dire consequences down the road. Don't wait till it's too late to heed the warning. Take care of business (it's your life) and be around to enjoy the payoff.

Facing the facts. Some events are so far-flung that the chance of their happening is as likely as sighting a black swan. The truth is that some people also adopt this philosophy in life. Why purchase disability insurance? Who needs a will? Chances are it'll never happen — until it does. Some eternal optimists never see a cloud in the sky. As such, they fail to anticipate downside risks or the need to save for a rainy day. Then, if something unexpected occurs, it creates havoc in their life. That's why they make umbrellas.

Putting all your eggs in one basket. If you place all your eggs in one basket, any fall will be a messy one. This truism applies, for example, in cases where one client represents too great a percentage of your company's sales, where most of your money is concentrated in a handful of investments, or even where all your attention is devoted to a single job opportunity at the expense of other promising job search situations. The fact is, even if everything looks rosy today, nothing in the world is a sure bet. Diversification protects you against downside risk.

IS IT WORTH THE GAMBLE?

People place small bets every day — such as running out to an appointment at the last minute or leaving home without an umbrella. Even though the consequences are small, you're still rolling the dice — sometimes you'll win, other times you'll lose. The danger is that after you get a few small wins under your belt, you'll develop a false sense of security and feel you can double down. It's very easy to convince yourself that you're unbeatable. And, like a gambler, your bets get bigger and bigger . . . until you lose.

Did you ever stop and think of the effect that risk-taking is having on your life? For example, is the stress having an impact on your health? Are you losing needed sleep worrying about the future? Does your life feel like an emotional roller coaster?

Think of the consequences of your actions: What if the BIG bet doesn't go your way? How would the loss change your life? What would the loss mean to your family? What impact would the loss have on the relationships that you hold dear? Will you ever be able to recover from it?

So remind me again . . . why are you risking it all? Is it the thrill and the adrenaline rush? Are you trying to impress your friends? Does it make you feel better to have one more toy than your neighbor?

Living on the edge isn't the "be-all and end-all." It doesn't take a brain surgeon to realize that there are no guarantees in life — which means that playing the odds through excessive risk-taking is like playing with fire. Unfortunately, when you get burned, there may be serious consequences. As author Ray Bradbury once said, "Living at risk is jumping off the cliff and building your wings on the way down."

The key, then, is to take calculated risks and only place bets on things that you're willing to lose. As the saying goes, "Take risks: If you win, you will be happy; if you lose, you will be wise." Make sense? You bet.

A MARRIAGE
MADE IN
HEAVEN

Remember your first date with that special someone? You spent hours combing through your wardrobe, fixing your hair, and making sure that the food and ambiance were perfect. You staged the "event" like a producer would a Broadway show.

The day finally approached . . . It was a HUGE success. (BIG sigh.)

What was next? Anticipation (LOTS of it) . . .

Your mind replayed every moment of the date more times than reruns of *The Brady Bunch*. "Did he have as good a time as I had?" "Should I call her now or would it be too pushy?" "I didn't say that, did I?" You couldn't seem to get him out of your head even if you tried, but who's trying? Thinking of her made your heart pound so loudly that you wondered if others could hear it.

More dates. More laughs. More good times. And then it finally happened . . . commitment.

"I, (bride/groom), take you (groom/bride), to be my (husband/wife), to have and to hold from this day forward, for better or for worse, for richer, for poorer, in sickness and in health, to love and to cherish, from this day forward until death do us part."

Upon reflection, it's abundantly clear that your entire world revolved around your partner during the courtship phase of the relationship. Yet, as time passes, it's not unusual for other priorities to sneak in — in fact, some folks may even take their spouse for granted, or at least act that way. Whatever happened to "from this day forward until death do us part"?

WHAT MAKES RELATIONSHIPS LAST?

Basic elements of a successful relationship include sharing common interests, communicating on a regular basis, displaying appreciation and affection, embracing intimacy, and showing real empathy. Honesty, trust, respect, and fidelity are also critical ingredients. Importantly, while the presence of these factors won't necessarily enhance the relationship, because they're expected, the absence of any of these qualities can turn a marriage from "heavenly" to . . . well, you know.

While best intentions are all good, your daily actions form the foundation of any successful relationship. As someone once said, "Watch your thoughts, for they become words. Watch your words, for they become actions. Watch your actions, for they become habits. Watch your habits, for they become your character. And watch your character, for it becomes your destiny!" This logic also applies to successful relationships. Actions become habits, which ultimately determine the destiny of your relationship. Here are some positive actions worthy of your consideration:

It's about us. Be mindful that your focus should shift from me to us and from mine to ours. That being said, it's still important to build a life together without surrendering your identity.

Be tolerant. Your spouse isn't perfect. (Neither are you.) Accept your spouse for who he or she is, rather than the person you want him or her to be.

Communicate. Practice active listening, thoughtful speaking, and constructive dialogue. Remember that silence and attention can be forms of communication, too.

Compromise, compromise, compromise. Know what's important to your spouse. Keep your spouse's needs in mind at all times and try to be accommodating whenever possible.

Don't keep score. Be prepared to go the extra mile. Successful relationships don't have a winner and a loser. You both win or lose together.

Pull your weight. A relationship doesn't require a boss. Each participant should share responsibilities appropriately based on the strengths and goals of each individual.

Manage life's ups and downs. Adversity is inevitable. The key is how you deal with it. First, acknowledge that your spouse has good intentions. Second, focus your discussions on the issue — without withdrawing, hurling insults, or getting personal. Most importantly, be supportive when the chips are down. As Oprah Winfrey once said, "Lots of people want to ride with you in the limo, but what you want is someone who will take the bus with you when the limo breaks down."

Keep the romance alive. Find happiness simply being in the presence of one another. As the years go by, build shared experiences and find ways to add spice to your life. Never take the relationship for granted.

Make your relationship a priority. Find balance between work and family, acknowledging that both contribute to your happiness and the strength of your relationship.

Grow older and wiser together. The most exciting part of a long-standing relationship is the growth that you achieve together, building on the promise of your marriage vows into fuller, more capable people joined through love and shared commitment.

Shared beliefs and values form the heart of every successful relationship and ultimately determine its success. If any of your spouse's viewpoints are the polar opposite of yours, that can make your life together difficult. The key is to understand your spouse's viewpoint and agree on the best way to move forward, which may involve additional time or enlisting the help of a trusted friend or counselor. The alternative is sweeping the issue under the carpet and waiting till it rears its ugly head. Some areas where good people may differ:

Family. Do you want to have children or remain childless? Do you prefer to have a small or a large family?

Money matters. Are you a spender or a saver? How much sacrifice are you willing to make today to ensure a bright future?

Risk. How much risk are you willing to accept?

Faith. How much significance does religion play in your life?

Togetherness. How much time do you need alone or with "the guys" or "the girls"? How much time would you like to spend with your spouse versus with other couples?

Change. Do you prefer the familiar or relish change?

Roots. Are you open to moving to a different town or do you prefer remaining close to friends and family?

Decisions. Do you believe "major" decisions should be made individually or jointly?

Priorities. Do you strive for balance between home and work?

Desires. Whose needs do you place first, yours or your spouse's?

There are very few things in life as rewarding as having a soul mate. You'll have someone who cheers you on to greatness, provides a shoulder to cry on, and helps you conquer the world. That'll make celebrations more enjoyable and setbacks more bearable. Having a soul mate will bring out the very best in you, making you the person you want to be rather than the person you are. In fact, you'll know your soul mate as well as the person in the mirror. Over time, you'll communicate with your soul mate without even uttering a word. That'll make it seem as though there's no challenge too large, no problem too insurmountable, and no dream unattainable as long as you have your soul mate by your side.

Sure, every relationship requires commitment and hard work. But it's absolutely worth it! So never stop courting your spouse. And you'll be among the lucky couples who live happily ever after.

NEVER STOP COURTING YOUR SPOUSE. AND YOU'LL BE AMONG THE LUCKY COUPLES WHO LIVE HAPPILY EVER AFTER.

FRANK SONNENBERG

TOUGH LOVE: A LIFELONG GIFT

Why are cheating, stealing, lying, and bullying so prevalent today? Don't folks know the difference between right and wrong? More importantly, don't they care? You have to wonder if life would be this way if the offenders had received a dose of tough love while they were young.

Here are some common scenarios that occur every day:

- "I let him run around during dinner because *I don't have the heart to discipline him.*"

- "We won't make her bring the stolen item back to the store because *it's not that expensive.*"

- "We didn't punish him for getting into the fight, because *kids will be kids.*"

- "I didn't confront him after he got caught cheating because *everyone does it.*"

- "We let her go out with him even though he spells trouble because *we can't pick her friends.*"

Sometimes, we think we're doing our kids a favor by giving them space, avoiding confrontation, or covering for their misdeeds. We justify our actions by not wanting to make a scene in public or because we need some personal downtime after a tough day. The truth is, even though our excuses may seem "valid" in that moment, actions or non-actions have consequences.

If our kids don't learn the difference between right and wrong when they're young, bad behavior will eventually turn into bad habits that are impossible to break.

A LITTLE TOUGH LOVE GOES A LONG WAY

Nurturing is a parent's responsibility. Parents must teach their kids the difference between right and wrong. This is not a role to be delegated to others. These lessons shape character and form the foundation of a child's conscience — a guiding force through life. Behind every good kid is a parent or caregiver who understands the importance of raising the child that way.

The buck stops with you. Everyone must be responsible and accountable for their actions. Good behavior should be celebrated and bad behavior disciplined. No one should receive a pass. This applies to all folks, whether they are prominent and successful or not and regardless of whether we like them personally. Remember, if we don't address bad behavior, we are implicitly encouraging it through our inaction.

Excuses are no excuse. We must stop tolerating poor behavior. Period. We can't "let someone off the hook" because it's convenient or because we dislike confrontation. Furthermore, excuses noting the "small size" of the infraction or that "everyone does it" don't cut it anymore. Right is right and wrong is wrong. When we blur the difference between right and wrong, we create confusion and minimize the significance of poor behavior.

Actions must have consequences. Positive and negative reinforcement should be timely and consistent. Likewise, punishments should be commensurate with the "crime." Tough love is not easy to dole out, but there are times when it's necessary. Saying "no" to your child, when warranted, can be tantamount to an act of love.

Role models play an important role. Every time a revered role model exhibits inappropriate behavior, it may have an adverse impact on our kids and on society. The next time you question whether celebrities influence behavior, ask yourself why they are paid so handsomely to endorse products. The fact is, we should publicly shame role models who exhibit disgraceful behavior, while also letting their sponsors learn of our displeasure.

The rule of law. Rules and laws should be either enforced or eliminated. Furthermore, they should be fairly and equally applied to everyone. It's important to note that when enough people break rules and laws, those rules not only become meaningless — they also invite cynicism and defiance.

Speak up. When we turn a blind eye to poor behavior, we're enabling it. It's not enough for us to throw up our hands in disgust. It's time to speak up with conviction. Each and every voice matters.

Don't be an enabler. It's time to stop covering for someone because it's profitable! Enough with the spin! Anyone who promotes, covers for, or hides indiscretion is as guilty as those who commit these acts. You can't have it both ways. You're either for it or against it.

PROVE THAT YOU CARE

Next time you see someone cheat, steal, curse, or lie, remember that we're each partly to blame for the behavior. We continue to admire celebrities and athletes even though they live reckless lives; we continue to vote for corrupt politicians even after they disgrace their offices; and we accept excuses, turn a blind eye, and accept the shameful behavior of role models because we're either too apathetic or too lazy to call them out — or because it's more convenient for us to look the other way. The truth is, some of this behavior exists because we allow it to exist.

Some may believe we're doing people a favor by giving them a pass, but you be the judge: What incentive do these folks have to stop misbehaving? What are the chances that their "crime" will be even bigger next time? What do onlookers learn when offensive actions have no consequences? And, given their poor behavior, what chance do these offenders have to be successful in life if they don't change course?

It's time raise the bar; it's time to stand up for what's right; it's time to lift our collective conscience. We must not let our kids fall through the cracks. We must not let ourselves become desensitized to these ills. We must not shy away from our responsibilities. This runaway train must be stopped before it derails. While we may not be able to change the world, we can change the world around us. Begin today. It's time for tough love.

TRADITION: THE TRUE MEANING OF THE HOLIDAYS

When you hear the word *holiday*, what comes to mind? If you're like most people, shopping, parties, sales, and catalogs rank near the top of your list — while more shopping, parades, a day off, and football follow closely behind. Wouldn't you think that holidays would be more meaningful to us? The truth is, many holidays are becoming so commercialized that our proud traditions are in danger of becoming trivialized.

Think about it . . . we're so afraid of offending people that we ban any symbol with the slightest religious connection from our public spaces. ("Happy Holidays"? Humbug!) Today, we're so profit-motivated that we expect retail employees to abandon their family dinners to return to their store in time for the sale. Or worse yet, their employers force them to supervise "midnight madness" sales extravaganzas, featuring over-caffeinated shoppers seeking that "dream buy."

Many of us can't even remember the true meaning of the holidays. Memorial Day has morphed from remembering our fallen soldiers to the unofficial beginning of summer. Labor Day's role in recognizing the achievements of organized labor now just marks the end of summer and a return to school. Veterans Day is honored as a day off from work.

TRADITION: THE FOUNDATION OF OUR CULTURE

Traditions represent a critical piece of our culture. They help form the structure and foundation of our families and our society. They remind us that we are part of a history that defines our past, shapes who we are today and who we are likely to become. Once we ignore the meaning of our traditions, we're in danger of damaging the underpinning of our identity.

Unfortunately, this indifference isn't limited to holiday traditions. Many people don't treat American, family, or religious traditions with the same emphasis and respect afforded in years past. Family meals around the table have been reduced to eating on the fly. Soccer tournaments are scheduled on Father's Day — heaven forbid our kids trade game time for quality family time. Reading before bedtime has given way to "vegging" in front of the TV, so that parents have their downtime. Family vacations have been known to include bringing a nanny along on the trip to "entertain" the kids.

TRADITION PERFORMS AN IMPORTANT ROLE IN OUR SOCIETY

- Tradition contributes a sense of comfort and belonging. It brings families together and enables people to reconnect with friends.
- Tradition reinforces values such as freedom, faith, integrity, a good education, personal responsibility, a strong work ethic, and the value of being selfless.
- Tradition provides a forum to showcase role models and celebrate the things that really matter in life.
- Tradition offers a chance to say "thank you" for the contribution that someone has made.
- Tradition enables us to showcase the principles of our Founding Fathers, celebrate diversity, and unite as a country.
- Tradition serves as an avenue for creating lasting memories for our families and friends.
- Tradition offers an excellent context for meaningful pause and reflection.

TRADITION: THE HEART OF OUR CULTURE

As leaders, role models, and parents, we must strive to utilize every opportunity available to us to reinforce the values and beliefs that we hold dear. Whether it's reciting the Pledge of Allegiance before school, saying grace before a meal, reading our children a story before bedtime, orienting new employees with a discussion of the company's beliefs and values, talking to our kids about our heroes and role models, providing quality feedback during an employee performance review, having the weekly family pancake breakfast on Sunday, or asking business colleagues to attend the "Race for the Cure" — no moment is too small or insignificant in the quest to convey the true meaning of the traditions and the values that unite us. Once these values are internalized, they affect the norms that influence our day-to-day actions, determine what's important, reinforce appropriate behavior, and change attitudes toward ourselves and our relationships with others.

That's where traditions come in. We should emphasize the sportsmanship and determination of our athletes as much as we underscore winning during the Olympics. We should fulfill a Secret Santa wish for a family in need just as we satisfy the holiday wishes of our own family and friends. We should emphasize what a person did to help others in his/her career ascent as much as we celebrate the personal achievements of a retiree. We should renew our vows to our spouse as much as we shower him or her with gifts on wedding anniversaries. We should emphasize the struggles that people endured for the right to vote as much as we ask people to support a candidate. We should spotlight how celebrities conduct themselves in their *personal lives* as much as we celebrate their *professional* achievements at the awards ceremony.

The alternative to action is taking these values for granted. The result is that our beliefs will get so diluted, over time, that our way of life will become foreign to us. It's like good health. You may take it for granted until you lose it. If we disregard our values, we'll open our eyes one day and won't be able to recognize "our world" anymore. The values that support the backbone of our country, our family, and our faith will have drifted for so long that the fabric of our society will be torn.

Don't let thoughtless apathy overshadow tradition. We all have a moral obligation to regularly remind the world why our values matter to us. Laws and regulations won't protect our culture. In fact, somebody recently figured out that we have concocted 35 million laws to enforce the Ten Commandments. So the next time you celebrate a holiday, remember that your real gift and responsibility is to mark the true meaning of the day. Cheers!

KIDS DON'T COME WITH AN INSTRUCTION MANUAL

O ne day you have a baby and the next day you're bringing him or her home. Okay . . . now what?

Sure, we've all been kids and vaguely remember our childhood, but that's not a very good rehearsal for the real thing — parenthood. Becoming a parent is a little scary. No, . . . it's VERY scary. On one hand, you feel like you've been thrown into the pool without first learning how to swim. On the other hand, being put to the test is a small price to pay for parenthood — one of the most exhilarating and rewarding experiences of a lifetime.

As parents, we want the very best for our kids: to lead happy, healthy, and productive lives. We want our kids to live up to their potential, to grow up to be decent human beings, and to contribute back to society. And, although these goals are very admirable, getting across the finish line isn't always easy. For instance, when our kids fall down, we feel their pain; when our kids lose, we lose with them; and when our kids get rejected, we feel their disappointment.

As loving parents, we make every effort to guide our kids to the Promised Land and shield them from dangers lurking around the bend. Unfortunately, sometimes our well-intentioned actions set us on a collision course with our kids. For example, we "coach" our kids not to make the same mistakes that we've made; we scrutinize our kids' activities to ensure that they're trying their best; and of course, we flip out when they really step out of bounds. Some people may say we're meddling; others call it hovering; our kids would probably say we're driving them crazy. The truth is, even though everything we do is out of our love for them, we can be our kids' worst nightmare.

NAG . . . NAG . . . NAG

Work hard. Although our kids aren't always willing participants, we try to instill a strong work ethic in them at an early age. "I know Johnny's parents don't make him clean up his room, but Johnny's not our child."

Do your best. We want our kids to understand that their work isn't finished until it's done "properly." So we send them back to the drawing board and ask them to raise their game. That doesn't always please them — especially when there's something good on TV.

Share your toys. Sharing is a very difficult concept for little children to learn. Come to think of it, it's a difficult concept for many adults to grasp also. Well, that doesn't stop us from trying to teach our kids right from wrong.

Reach for the stars. We want our kids to set stretch goals for themselves in life. So, just when our kids reach their comfort zone, we drive them crazy by suggesting that they have the potential to achieve more.

Values matter. I'm sure our kids get tired of hearing, "Always tell the truth," "Sit up straight," "Save for a rainy day," and "Don't talk with your mouth full" — but ask yourself, would you like to eat across from yourself?

Learn by your mistakes. It really hurts to watch our kids hit a wall after making a mistake. So it's tempting to overcompensate by trying to raise them in a bubble. I know, I know. Our kids won't be independent if we force them to ride through life with training wheels. Experience is a good teacher — we just hope they appreciate that when they get older.

You're judged by the company you keep. When our kids are young, we have total control over their environment. When they get older, however, their friends have a major influence on their lives. As the adage goes, "You're judged by the company you keep." We cross our fingers, hoping they choose wisely.

Eat your vegetables. Good luck trying to "preach" healthy living habits to a teenager who thinks French fries are a health food, who could be a gold-medal winner if video games were an Olympic sport, or who could be the poster child for "couch potato." The habits they grow up with may "shape" them for life. Sometimes that's a tough thing to swallow.

NO ONE'S PERFECT (NOT EVEN PARENTS)

A note to our kids:

Although we aim to do our best, we aren't perfect. So please try to understand. As your parents, it's our goal to never have a second agenda, an ulterior motive, or expect to be paid back — all we want is what's best for you. Period. That means that although we're not "cool" anymore, embedded in those recollections of the five-mile walks to school (uphill both ways), there are occasional lessons to be learned. Listen to us every once in a while — we may still know a thing or two about life, and we desperately want to share it with you.

We may not have all the answers, but I'm sure we can figure it out together. And since we've made our share of mistakes in life, learn from our missteps. Why run into the wall and get hurt when we've already "been there, done that"? And, if we're pushing you to live up to your potential or to be a better person, why put up a fight? Would you rather have parents who don't care?

We know that we get on your nerves sometimes. We know that it's your life to live. But we wouldn't be doing our "job" if we didn't get under your skin every once in a while. That's what parents do. One thing we can promise. We will ALWAYS be in your corner rooting for you. We will ALWAYS put your needs before our own. And we will ALWAYS be there to pick up the pieces if things head south. Remember, no one will ever love you more than we do.

Being a parent is a tough job. We're not complaining. We wouldn't have it any other way. We are so blessed and honored to be your parents. But unfortunately, parents aren't issued an instruction manual. By the time we really figure out this parenting thing, you'll be all grown up having children of your own. . . . Now it's your turn.

CHALLENGES

ARE ROLE MODELS BECOMING EXTINCT?

When we were growing up, our teachers saluted great individuals who changed the course of history; during dinnertime, our parents lovingly recalled their idols; and of course, we had our own personal heroes who walked on water.

Martin Luther King Jr., Princess Diana, Leonard Bernstein, Walter Cronkite, Colin Powell, Helen Keller, Ronald Reagan, Bill Gates, John Kennedy, Vince Lombardi, Steve Jobs, the Beatles, Tim Russert, John Glenn, Mother Teresa . . . to name a few.

There was something about these people that made them special. They led by example, raised the bar for us, and were simply the best of the best. We might have even wanted to be them, someday.

We looked up to them, and to other role models, because of their accomplishments, such as overcoming obstacles to achieve greatness, speaking up when no one else would, living rags-to-riches stories, being poster children for honesty and integrity, putting others' needs ahead of their own, and fighting tirelessly for causes they believed in. Many of these individuals changed our world . . . forever.

I know it's a generality, but would you be proud if your kids followed in the footsteps of many of today's politicians, professional athletes, Hollywood celebrities, or pop musicians? There's no need to mention them by name. You know who I'm talking about. Sure, there are some wonderful people to celebrate, but too many of today's public figures are train wrecks — purveyors of greed, recklessness, or dishonesty. Too often they're excused for drug and alcohol abuse, marital infidelity, and personal arrogance as we sit mesmerized by their fame. Need I say more?

I'm not suggesting that role models have to be saints, but let's get real. Many executives can't tell the difference between right and wrong until they're caught, many politicians appear to treat integrity as a liability, and celebrities live so close to the edge that many are in danger of falling off. Shame? Disgust? Public outrage? Nope. Too many journalists are no longer interested in reporting the facts; they're more concerned with ratings, shaping the news, or giving cover to those who subscribe to their personal views. Obviously, there's a void that needs to be filled.

That's where you come in. What can *you* do to serve as a role model?

BECOME PART OF THE SOLUTION

Hey, big shot. You don't have to be a celebrity or a superstar to be a role model. Chances are if you're a parent, teacher, coach, religious leader, or manager, you're influencing people every day. Make it positive!

Set the bar high. Have high expectations for others *and* yourself. Avoid the tendency to adjust the target downward just to accommodate mediocrity.

Inspire others. When you're a role model, every message you send is critical. For example, people will notice whether or not you value a good education, the relationship that you have with your spouse, how you work under pressure, how you behave during the Little League game, and whether you're confident enough to admit fault. Don't wait for the stars to align to demonstrate good behavior. Deliver your message every day in small ways.

Look in the mirror. Look to see if you're sending the wrong message. Here are some examples of behavior gone awry: cheating has become a substitute for hard work; you have become ruthless to get ahead; drugs are your rewards for success; life is about stuff, not people; relationships are disposable; the only thing that matters is winning.

Stand for something. Good role models are objective and fair. Furthermore, they have the strength of their convictions. They believe what they say and say what they believe. Mark Twain may have said it best, "Action speaks louder than words but not nearly as often."

Walk the talk. Ensure that your words and actions are consistent.

Integrity matters. Good role models are open, honest, and trustworthy. Make sure to finish what you start and follow through on commitments.

Be respectful. Treat others as you want to be treated.

Believe in yourself. Be confident in who you are and what you represent. But balance that confidence with a dose of humility.

Hold people accountable. Don't accept bad behavior. Speak up against abuses. If you don't condemn poor behavior, then you're a co-conspirator. Life isn't a spectator sport.

Nobody's perfect. Accept responsibility for your actions. When you make a mistake, admit fault and show you mean it by taking corrective action.

You're judged by the company you keep. Surround yourself with people of high character and integrity. They may rub off on you and provide extra encouragement when the stakes are high or the going gets tough.

Your soul is NOT for sale. Listen to your conscience. That's why you have one.

STEP UP TO THE CHALLENGE

Here's my bottom line. I don't care how famous you are or how much money or power you have. I don't care how many games you've won, how many records you've broken, or how many awards hang on your wall. The fact is, if you're a lousy role model, then you're a drag on society. Period. Your friends may excuse your behavior; your colleagues may laugh at your antics; and some people may conveniently look the other way to provide you with cover. None of that will change the reality.

But now it's time for all responsible people to take action. Yes, you! You don't have to be a powerful politician, famous actor, award-winning musician or an athlete in the big leagues to have fans. The truth is, you are influencing people every day. Be a positive force in their lives.

Every time you point someone in the right direction, you're not only making a distinctive contribution to his or her life . . . you're passing the torch to someone who'll likely pay it forward. Although it's very difficult to change the whole world, we can at least change the world around us. Your actions today represent the future for our kids. Remember, little footsteps in the sand usually follow larger ones, so watch where you step.

THE MANY FACES OF GREED

G reed is a term that describes ruthless people with naked ambition, people with an insatiable appetite for riches, those who give new meaning to the word *selfish*.

Greed evokes images of the rich and famous playing with lavish toys such as luxurious yachts, expensive furs, and mansions that resemble palaces. Think women dripping in diamonds and middle-aged men in expensive sports cars. To greedy people, it's as much about flaunting material trappings as it is about winning the game. As Gordon Gekko said in *Wall Street*, "It's not a question of enough, pal. It's a zero sum game, somebody wins, somebody loses."

It's critical, however, *not* to equate success and wealth with greed. The fact is, many successful people give generously of their wealth and/or their time. It's also true that you don't have to be particularly wealthy in order to be able to give. As Mother Teresa once said, "If you can't feed a hundred people, then feed one." People without means contribute generously of their time and skills every day, yet others don't.

Greed doesn't discriminate between rich and poor. There are many ways that greed rears its ugly head every day:

THE MANY FACES OF GREED

Life's a spectator sport. "Bystanders" who do everything they can to get out of work are greedy people. While colleagues work at a frantic pace, selfish people work hard to avoid working at all. They spend their days moving piles of papers on their desk while they watch everyone else go crazy. These guys wouldn't lift a finger if their life depended on it. When a job is complete, however, you can bet they'll be first in line to claim the rewards of the effort made (by someone else).

Gaming the system. Greedy people look for clever ways or loopholes to outsmart rules and regulations, designed to protect the system, for personal gain. Although their actions may be entirely legal, greedy people evade their responsibilities by offloading the costs to others. Examples include companies that incorporate in the Cayman Islands to avoid paying taxes and politicians who waste hard-earned taxpayer money by conducting "official business" at resort destinations.

It's all about me. *A Christmas Carol* is an 1843 tale about Ebenezer Scrooge, a stingy and greedy businessman who has no place in his life for kindness, compassion, charity, or benevolence. In modern times, you'll find that some wealthy business executives receive an obscene year-end bonus and lavish company benefits while telling employees that the company hasn't done well enough to support annual employee raises. Why? "Because I'm worth it." But catch them in a down year, and don't be surprised when they ask others to "share the pain."

You've got my vote (as long as it doesn't affect me). Greedy people have strong opinions about issues but expect others to shoulder the burdens. These hypocrites believe that our country should go to war, as long as we send someone else's kid; the deficit should be reduced, as long as it doesn't affect their pet projects; taxes should be raised, as long as the additional taxes don't affect their personal pocketbook.

Something for nothing. Greedy people are first in line to ask for more but last in line to make the effort required to earn the rewards. Instead of adopting the view that everyone benefits as the pie gets larger, they view the pie as a constant — there's only so much to go around. They feel they deserve a larger piece, even at someone else's expense, and they're going to take it.

Takes all kinds. Greedy people take things that don't belong to them even at the expense of friends or colleagues. This can take the form of bluffing their way to an unwarranted promotion or accepting credit for someone else's idea. They reason that if these losers aren't smart enough to take the spoils, then the losers don't deserve them.

Robbing someone's confidence. Some people bring out the best in others while selfish people focus on themselves. Greedy people make themselves feel better by tearing down other people rather than by helping others feel good about themselves. Greedy people have the ability to suck the oxygen right out of a room.

Borrowing from the future. Greedy people care about their needs today and kick problems down the road. They put band-aids on problems rather than solving the root cause; they buy things that benefit their organization today rather than investing in its future; they borrow to fund their buying addiction and stick others with the bill. Rather than taking the easy way out, parents, political leaders, executives, and the rest of us have a moral responsibility to provide a legacy for those who follow.

We are such a competitive society. We measure success by finishing in first place, making it to the top of our game, and having better toys than our neighbors. We value instant gratification by encouraging people to consume rather than to save for a rainy day — people borrow money to prove that they live large. We idolize people who drive expensive cars, wear the latest fashions, and live in luxurious homes. Greedy or not, we all help perpetuate the addiction.

THE MORE YOU GIVE, THE MORE YOU RECEIVE

When do we ever stress the importance and value of generosity over material wealth? The fact is, according to one of the longest-running social-science studies* of our time, helping others will lead to a beautiful life. Generous people believe that you gain more satisfaction in life from giving rather than taking. They've learned that greedy people are never satisfied that they have enough. They're like sharks that spend their entire life hunting and consuming. All the oceans in the world can't satisfy these eating machines.

Generous people give out of love, not obligation — without strings attached. Generous people know that a gift doesn't have to be momentous. It can be as simple as a smile. Giving doesn't have to be planned. Some of the best gifts in life are random acts of kindness such as creating a special moment for someone to remember. Giving doesn't have to be from your material wealth; it can be a gift from your heart. It can take the form of giving someone confidence and respect, slowing down enough to provide someone some quality time, or sharing an honest opinion. Giving doesn't have to provide an immediate benefit. You can give your children a strong sense of values, self-confidence, and a first-class education. Think about it: If enough people make a small gesture for someone else every day, we could transform the world. Do you spend more time giving or taking?

*Source: http://www.dailygood.org/view.php?qid=3089
One of the longest-running social-science studies on happiness occurred in the 1920s. It included semi-annual interviews of 200 people until participants graduated from high school, and continued to follow them at intervals of 10 years. An astounding 90 percent of people stayed in the study, offering tremendous insight into what constitutes a happy life. According to psychologist and researcher Paul Wink of Wellesley College, who oversees the study, one key finding is the ability to give to others. Paul Wink co-authored a book on the findings titled *In the Course of a Lifetime.*

ETHICS
AS USUAL

One of the first things we learn as children is the difference between right and wrong (the punishment being the time-out chair). Yet as we grow up, we too easily forget the simple lessons that we learned in kindergarten, and the line between acceptable and unacceptable behavior gets blurred.

This lack of ethical clarity — our inability to maintain rigorous standards of right and wrong — is not only confusing, it also erodes trust, damages relationships, destroys moral leadership, and weakens the fabric of our society. It's time to put an end to *ethics as usual* and restore our standards of decency and trust.

WHAT ARE THE CATALYSTS OF THIS BREAKDOWN?

Do as I say. While politicians create laws, many ignore them; while bosses create the rules, many subvert them; and while parents teach children values, many breach them. How can rules be taken seriously when the creators of the standards don't embrace the values they espouse?

To whom do the rules apply? The sad truth is that ethical standards are not applied equally. Athletes, actors, rock stars, politicians, and corporate chieftains serve as "role models" for our children. While we may find it entertaining when some of these people adopt "wild" lifestyles, society hails them for their performance while excusing their actions. Then we are appalled when our kids mimic their behavior.

At the same time, we continue to support politicians who come up short on ethical probes, tax audits, or standards of human decency. Yet as citizens, we get the book thrown at us if we neglect to pay a parking ticket on time. George Orwell got it right in *Animal Farm* when he wrote, "All animals are equal, but some are more equal than others." The fact is, we send mixed messages when some people are reprimanded for their actions, while the privileged few either buy their way out of a punishment or get off with a mere slap on the wrist.

The finish line keeps moving. How can we be expected to abide by a moral code of conduct when actions are inappropriate one day and appropriate the next? I clearly remember a time when foul language on TV set off alarm bells, yet over the years, it has become commonplace. Furthermore, even though we've learned that it's wrong to tell a lie, some "role models" believe that nuances such as a "white lie," exaggeration, or "spinning the truth" don't count.

The problem is that most of these infractions don't attract sufficient attention. Over time, however, the cumulative effect of these transgressions is significant — and the bar is lowered as a result.

Just don't get caught. Some people believe that an indiscretion is allowed as long as you don't get caught. When we try to evade individual responsibility by outsourcing our conscience to bureaucrats and pundits, our conscience begins to atrophy.

YOU'RE EITHER PART OF THE PROBLEM OR PART OF THE SOLUTION

Being a role model carries responsibility. If you're a teacher, clergyman, actor, executive, athlete, politician, or parent, people look up to you as a role model and imitate your behavior. Are you proud of the signals that you're sending? If not, it's time to get your act together! No one is asking you to be a saint, but living a life of commendable ethics and values is a good place to start.

Enough is enough. Where's your outrage? (Yes, you!) It's time that we stop excusing the unacceptable behavior of people masquerading as role models and expose them for what they really are — ethical derelicts. When people are held accountable for the wake of destruction they cause through ethical negligence, they'll have a choice — change their ways or face the consequences.

Stop looking the other way. Every person can make a difference by shining the spotlight on inappropriate behavior. In fact, according to psychological research, one person's opinion can sway the views of an entire group. The rationale is simple: People assume that if a lot of people do something, it must be "okay." That's because the autopilot switch in all of us instructs us to follow the crowd. It's well known that a herd mentality works best when a group is isolated from all external factors so that its members can't be influenced. (Think Jim Jones.) All it takes is one person to question the logic (in the company of others), and the entire group may begin to question the logic. Remember, if we don't expose the group's unacceptable behavior, we are condoning its actions.

Actions have consequences. If we don't hold people accountable for their behavior, we are creating a slippery slope. Understandably, it's difficult when the newly elected politician, most valuable player on the team, award-winning performer, or most-productive employee discredits the organization with his or her actions. We shouldn't have rules for one person and a different set for others. When we bend the rules and make "exceptions," norms shift and poor behavior can be viewed as acceptable.

Leaders must start leading. Leaders must live up to the definition of the term "leader." They must serve not only as positive role models themselves but must hold their colleagues accountable for their actions. The fact is, if a member of the organization commits an egregious act, it is a reflection on the violator and the organization the violator represents, as well as on the leader. If the leader defends an ethical deviant, turns a blind eye to the action, or sweeps the act under the rug, the behavior is condoned. This sends a signal to others that ethical standards are not priorities, and that short-term performance is more important than the reputation of the organization.

Your character matters most when nobody's looking. I long for the day when honor has meaning. In this world, most people do the right thing because they know that what goes around comes around. And if it doesn't, they know they'll get paid back in karma points.

In the new world I envision, people follow the spirit as well as the letter of the law. This is a world in which shaking someone's hand is as good as a contract and where one's reputation is a valued asset. This is a world in which people go to great lengths to protect their family name, and leaders see their first responsibility as strengthening the trust and credibility of their institutions. In this world, people do the right thing not only because it's considered acceptable behavior, but because they know that every action affects another action. In this world, bureaucracies don't police people because everyone sees it as their duty to call out unacceptable behavior — ethical derelicts are disgraced and shunned for their misdeeds. In this world, people are accountable to a higher power — themselves — letting their own conscience be their guide.

APATHY: WHO CARES?

I know there's work to do, but someone else will do it. Who cares if I pitch in; it always gets done anyway. Right?"

The truth is, some folks don't care about anything. They rarely get involved or pull their own weight. They have no work ethic, no sense of pride, and they invest just enough effort to squeak by. In fact, they're apathetic about most things in life. You could say they're among the living dead.

Some may ask, who cares if I'm apathetic? I'm not hurting anyone. But that's not really true. They're depriving themselves of the feeling of satisfaction that comes with caring; they're cheating *themselves* of the thrill of accomplishing something difficult; and they're robbing themselves of knowing that they've made a difference.

So who cares if you lead or follow, win or lose, or ever try your best? *You should!* Even if you have all the talent in the world, you're never going to amount to anything if you don't apply yourself. As Jimmy Buffett said, "Is it ignorance or apathy? Hey, I don't know and I don't care."

DO YOU HAVE A CARE IN THE WORLD?

What's turning you off? Is your apathy an isolated event or does it permeate many areas of your life? Is someone discouraging you or are you holding yourself back? Are you afraid of leaving your comfort zone? If you're in a rut, climb out.

Find your passion. "Force" yourself to find an interest. Get involved by making a small commitment. Volunteer. Assume a leadership role. After getting your feet wet and collecting a few small wins, jump in with both feet.

Be informed. If you want to earn the respect of others, it's important to remain informed. As the saying goes, "Try being informed instead of just opinionated."

Pay your dues. Manage your expectations. It takes many years to become an overnight success. Find ways to improve yourself every day.

Attitude matters. A positive attitude can make all the difference. See the glass as half full. Believe in your ability to make a difference.

IT'S NEVER TOO LATE TO CARE

Even though some folks show up, it's as though they're not even there. They're talented, but they don't apply themselves. They've got good ideas, but never voice them. They're born leaders, but choose to be followers. And even though they have dreams of grandeur, they choose to live an empty life of dependency.

The truth is, if you want to get anywhere, *you* have to make things happen. The world isn't going to beat a path to your door. It's easy to criticize others instead of sticking your neck out; it's painless to second-guess others from the sidelines instead of getting in the game; it's easy to blame others for your circumstances instead of accepting responsibility for your choices and actions. The fact is, *you* have the ability to fulfill your dreams — *if you care*.

I'm sure you remember the time you hit the ball out of the park. You made a suggestion and everyone smiled; you voiced your opinion and everyone applauded; you volunteered for the challenge and came out a star. Everyone was impressed. Most importantly, you made yourself proud because you knew you had the answer; you thought your opinion mattered; and you believed that you could make a difference by stepping forward — and you did! Once you know what it feels like to care, you'll never be apathetic again. As Helen Keller said, "Science may have found a cure for most evils; but it has found no remedy for the worst of them all — the apathy of human beings." The truth is, people who live without caring are people who are not truly living. Who cares? I hope you do.

EVEN IF YOU HAVE
ALL THE TALENT IN
THE WORLD,
YOU'RE NEVER
GOING TO AMOUNT
TO ANYTHING IF
YOU DON'T APPLY
YOURSELF.

FRANK SONNENBERG

RESOURCES

50 THINGS MONEY CAN'T BUY

1. Respect
2. Well-adjusted kids
3. Work-life balance
4. Natural beauty
5. Manners
6. Common sense
7. A clear conscience
8. Purpose in life
9. Integrity
10. Good friends
11. A long life
12. Close-knit family
13. An open mind
14. A worry-free day
15. Trust
16. A new beginning
17. Clean arteries
18. A great idea
19. An honest politician
20. Peace of mind
21. A good hair day
22. Patience
23. Luck
24. A good epitaph
25. Happy memories
26. Time to relax
27. A strong work ethic
28. A positive attitude
29. A happy home
30. Everything you may want
31. Good karma
32. Appreciation of the simple things
33. True love
34. A new shot at a missed opportunity
35. Peace in the world
36. A golden anniversary
37. Talent
38. A second chance in life
39. Quality time with your kids
40. Wisdom
41. Happiness
42. Humility
43. A good reputation
44. 25-hour day
45. Relationship with your kids
46. Youth
47. Class
48. Justice
49. A proper perspective
50. Selflessness

MAGIC
WORDS

Please • I'll try my best • You mean the world to me • You earned it
I'm sorry • That's what friends are for • I'll remember this forever
I'm listening • My mistake • You outdid yourself • It's already done
I volunteer • You come highly recommended • I'm wrong; you're right
We're in this together • I'm counting on you • I love you • You're a good
friend • Great job • You can do it • I trust you • I'm proud of you
Let's learn from this • What do you have to lose? • You made all the
difference • I'm so thankful • Finished • I accept responsibility • It's
your turn • Thank you • You can count on me • Let's share this • Do
your best • Good people finish first • Don't worry about it • A promise
is a promise • I'll do better next time • Let me help • You're welcome
Listen to your conscience • Let's shake on it • Pay it forward
Congratulations • Never forget • I'll get it this time • You're wonderful
Amen • I believe in you • Welcome home • You taught me well
Make it happen • Take a chance • It's my pleasure • It's your turn
I appreciate you

HOW TO BUILD TRUST AND CREDIBILITY

1. It takes many years to become an overnight success.
2. Good intentions are just the beginning.
3. Your reputation is their first impression.
4. Show people that you care about their needs.
5. A promise should be as binding as a contract.
6. Never sacrifice a long-term relationship for a short-term gain.
7. Don't expect people to look up to you if you look down on them.
8. Give credit where credit is due.
9. The danger of shooting from the hip is hitting yourself in the foot.
10. Be knowledgeable and remain current in your field.
11. Follow through on every commitment that you make.
12. Take the time to provide the rationale behind your recommendations.
13. Stay focused. Trying to be all things to all people is a guaranteed recipe for mediocrity.
14. Be objective.
15. Opinions held in secret never make a difference.
16. Never cut corners.
17. Stand up for the things that you believe in. (Waffles are for breakfast.)
18. Be a thought leader.
19. At the end of the day, you're judged by the value that you provide.
20. Be straight with people. Tell it like it is.
21. Don't be afraid to present bad news. It's worse to sweep it under the rug.
22. Remain calm, cool, and collected during difficult times.
23. Present both sides of an issue. (Let them judge for themselves.)
24. Be a good listener.
25. Disclose potential conflicts of interest.

26. Even a tiny exaggeration can destroy your credibility.
27. Once you make a decision, don't look back.
28. Always tell the truth or the truth will tell on you.
29. Surround yourself with people who have a high degree of integrity.
30. Your actions "off-stage" (e.g., at an office party or on Facebook) impact your trust and credibility.
31. Typos and grammatical errors loom larger than life.
32. Remain transparent. (You'll never be faulted for communicating too much.)
33. Never ask someone to do something that you're unwilling to do yourself.
34. Reliable and consistent behavior on your part allows people to anticipate what you'll do in the future.
35. Do what's right, even if nobody is looking.
36. You are judged by the company that you keep.
37. Your actions must match your words.
38. Being an expert in one area doesn't make you an expert in everything.
39. Admit when you're wrong.
40. Don't submit unfinished work as complete.
41. Never confuse quantity with quality.
42. Think before you open your mouth.
43. People who "hard sell" don't always have the facts on their side.
44. You gain more by making others look good than by singing your own praises.
45. Trying to be excellent in everything leads to mediocrity.
46. "Everybody does it" is a poor excuse for doing it yourself.
47. Words spoken in confidence are words spoken in trust.
48. Learn how to disagree without being disagreeable.
49. Repeating a rumor is as vicious as starting one.
50. People will test you in small ways before trusting you outright.
51. The only thing worse than talking about others is talking about yourself.
52. Great talent means nothing if you're not dependable.
53. Few people will fault you for being tough, if you're fair.
54. It's not only what you bring to the table but how you serve it.
55. REMEMBER, trust and credibility take years to develop but can be lost in seconds.

TRUST IS NEVER
GUARANTEED, AND
IT CAN'T BE WON
OVERNIGHT. TRUST
MUST BE CAREFULLY
CONSTRUCTED,
VIGOROUSLY NURTURED,
AND CONSTANTLY
REINFORCED.

FRANK SONNENBERG

TAKE THE PARENT PLEDGE

I PROMISE TO INSTILL THESE VALUES IN MY CHILDREN:

People look up to you — so don't let them down. | Real beauty is more than skin deep. | Make memories that you'll cherish forever. | Do your best, or don't do it. Make healthy choices — you only have one body. Learn something new every day. | Make a difference in someone's life. Turn barriers into hurdles. | Treat people the way you want to be treated. Your reputation is like a shadow — it will follow you everywhere. Establish priorities or you'll be overwhelmed by details. | Leave your comfort zone and color outside the lines. | Be honest with others and yourself. | Listen to your conscience. | Keep the faith. | Save for a rainy day or face stormy times ahead. | Give more than you take. | Invest your time rather than spending it. | Make someone feel special every day. Forget the failure — keep the lesson. | Tell the truth or the truth will tell on you. | Don't let success go to your head. | While effort matters, results count. | Remember your roots. | What you do speaks louder than what you say. | Get real — be yourself. | Don't take yourself too seriously. | Set ambitious goals that are realistic and achievable. | Work hard — work smart. | Find the sunshine behind every cloud. | Live your life with gusto. Help those who cannot help themselves. | If you're not proud, you're not finished. | Trust takes a long time to develop but can be destroyed in seconds. Give unconditional love. | Don't stress over things that you'll forget in five years. Don't ask someone to do something that you wouldn't do yourself. | Don't just talk — communicate. | The small things make the biggest difference. | It's one thing to dream, and quite another to make it happen. | Strive for excellence, not perfection. | Your promise should be as binding as a contract. | You can't demand respect — you must earn it. Hate is a cancer in one's soul. | Moderation is the balance in life. | Trying to be excellent at everything leads to mediocrity. | An ounce of love outweighs a pound of promises. | Always give 110% — it's the extra 10% that everyone remembers. | When you open your heart, you open your mind. | Work hard — play hard. | Where you've come from is less important than where you're going. | If you try to please the world, you'll never please yourself. | Congratulate yourself for a job well done. | If you believe you can't, you won't.

HOW TO LOSE TRUST AND CREDIBILITY

1. Act nice only when you need something.
2. Base decisions on bad or incomplete information.
3. Fake an answer rather than admitting you don't know.
4. Claim to be an expert in everything.
5. Fail to stand behind your product.
6. Tell two people two different stories.
7. Make self-serving recommendations.
8. Fail to follow up promptly.
9. Make careless mistakes or errors.
10. Show lack of care and concern.
11. Overpromise and underdeliver.
12. Bury information in the fine print.
13. Spin the truth.
14. Adopt a messy physical appearance.
15. Offer each customer a different price.
16. Love you before a sale; leave you afterward.
17. Recommend more than needed.
18. Show up late or miss deadlines.
19. Sell what you have — not what's needed.
20. Be inaccessible.
21. Speak in jargon.
22. Make excuses rather than accept responsibility.
23. Fail to fix a problem, promptly.
24. Disparage the competition or bad-mouth your own organization.
25. Compromise your principles and values.

26. Waffle on decisions.
27. Pass the buck.
28. Say one thing, do another.
29. Leave out important details.
30. Exaggerate or cry wolf.
31. Fail to present both sides of an issue.
32. Present boilerplate solutions to unique problems.
33. Expect others to do what you wouldn't do.
34. Show favoritism, strong bias, or prejudice.
35. Bully someone "smaller" than you.
36. Let someone learn about a problem through the grapevine.
37. Accept credit even though it's undeserved.
38. Misunderstand the needs of your audience.
39. Plagiarize.
40. Fail to answer questions clearly.
41. Make rules, but don't follow them.
42. Cast blame at the first sign of a problem.
43. Sweep problems under the rug.
44. Play politics rather than doing what's right.
45. Be inconsistent, unreliable, or unpredictable.
46. Run from tough decisions.
47. Change the terms of an agreed-upon deal.
48. Jump to a conclusion before knowing the facts.
49. Have an ulterior motive.
50. Hand in unfinished work as complete.

ALTHOUGH TRUST
TAKES A LONG TIME
TO DEVELOP, IT CAN
BE DESTROYED BY A
SINGLE ACTION.
MOREOVER, ONCE
LOST, IT IS VERY
DIFFICULT TO
RE-ESTABLISH.

FRANK SONNENBERG

WAYS
TO SAY
YOU CARE

I'm so proud of you. • Don't worry. Tomorrow's another day. • How could I forget? • Is there anything that I can do for you? • I'd like to make a toast… • We were so worried about you. • I'd prefer that you have it. It's obvious that you put a lot of time into this. • Sure I have time to talk. Your effort is never taken for granted. • If it's good enough for you, it's good enough for me. • That color looks great on you. • You exceeded our wildest expectations. • We couldn't have done it without you. • We'll miss you so much. • You're in our thoughts and prayers. • We'll always be here for you. • Your effort clearly shows. • Take half of mine. • I'm happy to teach you how to do it. • I'll never forget what you did for me. • What's your opinion? • It's my pleasure to introduce you… • I thought you'd be interested in this. • You made my day. • What can I do to help? • I'm so sorry. • I missed you. • I've learned so much from you. • I've always looked up to you. • I understand what you're going through. • Here, have mine. • You made all the difference. • You're going to be a star. Congratulations! • I've never seen anything this good. • Pay it forward. Do you want to talk? • I completely understand what you're saying. It's been too long since we talked. • I always have time for you. • Go get 'em! • It's the least we can do for you. • I'm so happy for you. • You're a good friend. • I love you. • If anyone can do it, you can. • Tell me all about it. • You do that so much better than I do. • Please be our guest. • Would you like to join us? • Let me show you. • Surprise! • You're one of a kind. • You changed my life.

IT'S THE LITTLE THINGS THAT COUNT

1. Remember their name.
2. Compliment them in public.
3. Pick up the tab.
4. Share the credit.
5. Ask if they're feeling better.
6. Follow up on their purchase.
7. Give a firm handshake.
8. Offer the last piece.
9. Lend an ear.
10. Come in under budget.
11. Confirm it's a convenient time to talk.
12. Bolster their confidence.
13. Pay it forward.
14. Leave your door open.
15. Give up your seat.
16. Show them the ropes.
17. Offer constructive feedback.
18. Pass on something of interest.
19. Offer an alternative solution.
20. Send a congratulatory note.
21. Provide an unsolicited recommendation.
22. Pick up after yourself.
23. Return it on time.
24. Offer without being asked.
25. Confirm the conversation.
26. Call for no reason.
27. Remember your last conversation.
28. Make them look good.
29. Answer them promptly.
30. Do the unexpected.
31. Give your undivided attention.
32. Listen before talking.
33. Steer the conversation to them.
34. Make it win-win.
35. Talk things through.
36. Remember special occasions.
37. Give without being asked.
38. Keep your advice to yourself, unless asked.
39. Arrive early.
40. Accept their advice.
41. Meet them halfway.
42. Don't keep score.
43. Make them feel special.
44. Tell it like it is.
45. Look at them when talking.
46. Exceed their expectations.
47. Show that you care.
48. Reach out if they're in need.
49. Let them go first.
50. Ask if they need anything, to save them the trip.

FRANK SONNENBERG

ABOUT THE AUTHOR

Frank Sonnenberg is a longtime champion of character and integrity. He is the author of five books and over 300 articles. His last book, *Managing With a Conscience*, was named one of the top business books of the year (2012).

Sonnenberg has been a strong advocate of trust and integrity in business and is a well-recognized expert in the area of personal values and responsibility. Notable accolades include:

- Named one of "America's Top 100 Thought Leaders" by *Trust Across America* (2014)

- Nominated as one of "America's Most Influential Small Business Experts" (2012)

- Named one of the "Top 75 Human Business Champions" (2014)

Additionally, *FrankSonnenbergOnline* was named among the "Best 21st Century Leadership Blogs" (2014).

Frank was formerly the National Director of Marketing for Ernst & Young's Management Consulting Group for over a decade. Sonnenberg and his firm have consulted to some of the largest and most respected companies in the world.

Sonnenberg has served as a columnist for *The Journal of Business Strategy*, as an expert panelist for *Bottom Line Business*, and on the editorial board of *The Journal of Training and Development*. He has also served on several boards.

CPSIA information can be obtained at www.ICGtesting.com
Printed in the USA
BVOW03s0216041214

377902BV00011B/108/P